I0530944

IDENTITY:
STICKING TO YOUR FAITH IN A PULL-APART WORLD

A Study of Ezra, Nehemiah, Esther, Daniel, Haggai, Zechariah, and Malachi

These last seven Old Testament books show you how to say "No" to the destructive influences of our world.

MELANIE NEWTON

JOYFUL WALK BIBLE STUDIES

Identity: Sticking to Your Faith in a Pull-Apart World—A Study of Ezra, Nehemiah, Esther, Daniel, Haggai, Zechariah, and Malachi

© 2025 by Melanie Newton. All rights reserved.

Published by Joyful Walk Press. Flower Mound, TX.

ISBN: 979-8-9925750-1-9

For questions about the use of this study guide or for bulk orders, please email us at melanienewton.com/contact.

The hand holding the ID card graphic on the cover was purchased from © Can Stock Photo / Abscent. The mottled purple background image was adapted from a public domain image available at pixabay.com (purple-608575.jpg by spicetree687).

Scripture quotations are taken from the Holy Bible, New International Version ®, NIV ®. Copyright © 1973, 1978, 1984 by International Bible Society. Used by permission of Zondervan Publishing Company. All rights reserved.

Melanie Newton is the author of "Graceful Beginnings" books for anyone new to the Bible and "Joyful Walk Bible Studies" for established Christians. Her mission is to help women learn to study the Bible for themselves and to grow their Bible-teaching skills to lead others.

Joyful Walk Bible Studies are grace-based studies for women of all ages. Each study guide follows the inductive method of Bible study (observation, interpretation, application) in a warm and inviting format.

We pray that you and your group will find *Identity: Sticking to Your Faith in a Pull-Apart World Bible Study* to be a resource that God will use to strengthen you in your faith walk with Him.

Christ-Focused • Bible-Rich • Grace-Based

JOYFUL WALK PRESS
Flower Mound, TX

MELANIE NEWTON

Melanie Newton is a Louisiana girl who made the choice to follow Jesus while attending LSU. She and her husband Ron married and moved to Texas for him to attend Dallas Theological Seminary. They stayed in Texas where Ron led a wilderness camping ministry for troubled youth for many years. Ron now helps corporations with their challenging employees and is the author of the top-rated business book, *No Jerks on the Job*.

Melanie jumped into raising three Texas-born children and serving in ministry to women at her church. Through the years, the Lord has given her opportunity to do Bible teaching and to write grace-based Bible studies for women that are now available from her website (melanienewton.com) and on Bible.org. *Graceful Beginnings* books are for anyone new to the Bible. *Joyful Walk Bible Studies* are for maturing Christians.

Melanie Newton loves to help women learn how to study the Bible for themselves. She also teaches online courses for women to grow their Bible-teaching skills to help others—all with the goal of getting to know Jesus more along the way. Her heart's desire is to encourage you to have a joyful relationship with Jesus Christ so you are willing to share that experience with others around you.

"Jesus took hold of me in 1972, and I've been on this great adventure ever since. My life is a gift of God, full of blessings in the midst of difficult challenges. The more I have learned and experienced God's absolutely amazing grace, the more I have discovered my faith walk to be a joyful one. I'm still seeking that joyful walk every day."

Melanie

OTHER BIBLE STUDIES BY MELANIE NEWTON

Graceful Beginnings books for anyone new to the Bible:

A Fresh Start (basics for new Christians)
Painting the Portrait of Jesus (the Gospel of John)
The God You Can Know (the character of God)
Grace Overflowing (an overview of Paul's 13 letters)
The Walk from Fear to Faith (7 Old Testament women)
Satisfied by His Love (women who knew Jesus)
Seek the Treasure (study of Ephesians)
Pathways to a Joyful Walk (6 pathways to a life filled with joy)

Joyful Walk Bible Studies for growing Christians:

Adorn Yourself with Godliness (1 Timothy and Titus, also in Spanish)
Everyday Women, Ever Faithful God (Old Testament women, also in Spanish)
Connecting Faith to Life on Planet Earth (Genesis 1-11; Revelation)
Graceful Living (the essentials for a grace-based Christian life)
Graceful Living Today (a devotional journal for a joyful life)
Healthy Living (Colossians and Philemon)
Heartbreak to Hope (the Gospel of Mark)
Identity: Sticking to Your Faith in a Pull-Apart World (Ezra thru Malachi)
Knowing Jesus, Knowing Joy (Philippians, also in Spanish)
Live Out His Love (New Testament women)
Perspective (1and 2 Thessalonians)
Profiles of Perseverance (Old Testament men, also in Spanish)
Radical Acts (Acts)
Reboot, Renew, Rejoice (1 and 2 Chronicles)
The God-Dependent Woman (2 Corinthians)
To Be Found Faithful (2 Timothy)

Resources for leading others

Be a Christ-Focused Small Group Leader
Leap into Lifestyle Disciplemaking
Bible Study Leadership Made Easy (online video course)
Painting the Picture of Jesus (the "I Am's" of Jesus lessons for children)
Teaching Children the God They Can Know (the character of God for children)

Download our catalogue and get resources for your spiritual growth at melanienewton.com.

Contents

Introduction

USING THIS STUDY GUIDE

This study guide consists of 11 lessons that cover the last seven Old Testament books to be written—Daniel, Ezra, Nehemiah, Esther, Haggai, Zechariah, and Malachi. The historical period is the Babylonian exile and the Jews' return to their homeland to rebuild and resettle. We will study these books in chronological order. The lessons are divided into 4 daily sections (about 25 minutes in length). If you cannot do the entire lesson one week, please read some of the Bible passages covered by the lesson.

Each lesson includes core questions that will take you through the process of inductive Bible study—observation, interpretation, and application. The process is more easily understood in the context of answering these questions:

- What does the passage say? *(Observation: What's actually there)* These will help you to notice all the information that is given in the text.

- What does it mean? *(Interpretation: The author's intended meaning)*

- How does this apply to me today? *(Application: making it personal)* The **Application for Today** section encourages you to look at similarities between what happened in the Scriptures and what you experience in today's world. You will be asked to find New Testament verses that apply to that similar situation.

STUDY ENHANCEMENTS

Additional Reading (optional): Embedded within the sections are suggestions for additional reading of chapters skipped in the lesson and outside sources of information.

Additional research you do for this lesson: At the end of each lesson, we left room for you to do your own research of anything in the lesson that was not covered in the questions.

Study Aids: To aid in proper interpretation and application of the study, five additional study aids are located where appropriate in the lesson:

- Historical Insights
- Scriptural Insights
- From the Hebrew (definitions of Hebrew words)
- Focus on the Meaning
- Think About It (thoughtful reflection)
- Maps and charts (at the end of the study guide)

Other useful study tools:

- *Blueletterbible.org* (or "Blue Letter Bible app) is especially helpful) to find cross references (verses with similar content to what you are studying) and meanings of the original Hebrew words or phrases used (usually called "interlinear"). You can also look at any verse in various Bible translations to help with understanding what it is saying.

- *Soniclight.com* is the website hosting *Dr. Tom Constable's Study Notes* on every book of the Bible, graciously provided by this much-loved professor at Dallas Theological Seminary. This is a great resource for additional research on any book we study—historical information, word meanings, scriptural insights, and discussion of difficult topics.

PODCASTS

Find podcasts for these lessons at melanienewton.com/podcasts (choose "18: Ezra to Malachi) and on most podcast providers. Or you can read the blogs associated with the podcasts at melanienewton.com/blog. Choose Ezra to Malachi category then scroll to find the title you want. Listen to the first podcast as an introduction to the study.

OLD TESTAMENT SUMMARY

About 1700 years after God created everything, He sent judgment on a rebellious race through a worldwide Flood. He later separated the nations with different languages and scattered them from Babel. Abraham, Isaac, and Jacob were founding fathers of the Hebrew people.

Sold into slavery, Joseph became a powerful foreign leader paving the way for his relatives to move to Egypt. The Israelites grew in number for ~400 years in Egypt but became slaves of the Egyptian rulers. So God delivered them from bondage through Moses who took the people across the Red Sea and taught them God's Law at Mt. Sinai. Joshua led the Israelites into the Promised Land after a 40-year trek in the wilderness because of their unbelief.

During the transition toward monarchy, there were deliverer-rulers called "Judges," the last of whom was Samuel. The first three Hebrew kings—Saul, David, and Solomon—each ruled 40 years. Under Rehoboam, the Hebrew nation divided into northern and southern kingdoms, respectively called Israel and Judah. Prophets warned against worshipping the foreign god Baal.

After the reign of 19 wicked kings in the north, Assyria conquered and scattered the northern kingdom. In the south, 20 kings ruled for ~350 years, until Babylon took the people into captivity for 70 years.

Zerubbabel, Ezra, and Nehemiah led the Jews back into Jerusalem over a 100-year period. More than 400 "silent years" spanned the gap between Malachi and Matthew.

The 39 books in the Old Testament are divided into 4 main categories:

- "The Law" (5 books)—the beginning of the nation of Israel as God's chosen people; God giving His Laws to the people that made them distinct from the rest of the nations.

- "History" (12 books)—narratives that reveal what happened from the time the people entered the Promised Land right after Moses died until 400 years before Christ was born.

- "Poetry & Wisdom" (5 books)—take place at the same time as the history books but are set apart because they are written as poems and have a lot of wise teaching in them.

- "Prophets" (17 books)—concurrent with the books of history and, except for Lamentations, reflect the name of the prophet through whom God spoke to the nation of Israel.

OLD TESTAMENT TIMELINE

This chart covers the time periods covered by the study lessons. The chart on the next page shows where each book fits in the Old Testament categories mentioned above.

Historical Period	Years B.C.	Book
The Babylonian Exile	605 – 538 B.C.	Jeremiah, Daniel, Ezekiel
Israel's return to the land and rebuilding the temple	538 – 520 B.C.	Ezra 1-6, Haggai, Zechariah
Jews staying outside of Israel	538 B.C. onward	Esther
More Jews return with Ezra	458 B.C.	Ezra 7-10
Rebuilding the walls of Jerusalem	445 – 432 B.C.	Nehemiah
The last writing of the Old Testament	432 - 431 B.C.	Malachi
The "silent years"	430 – 6 B.C.	*Ends in Luke 1 with the announcement of John's birth*

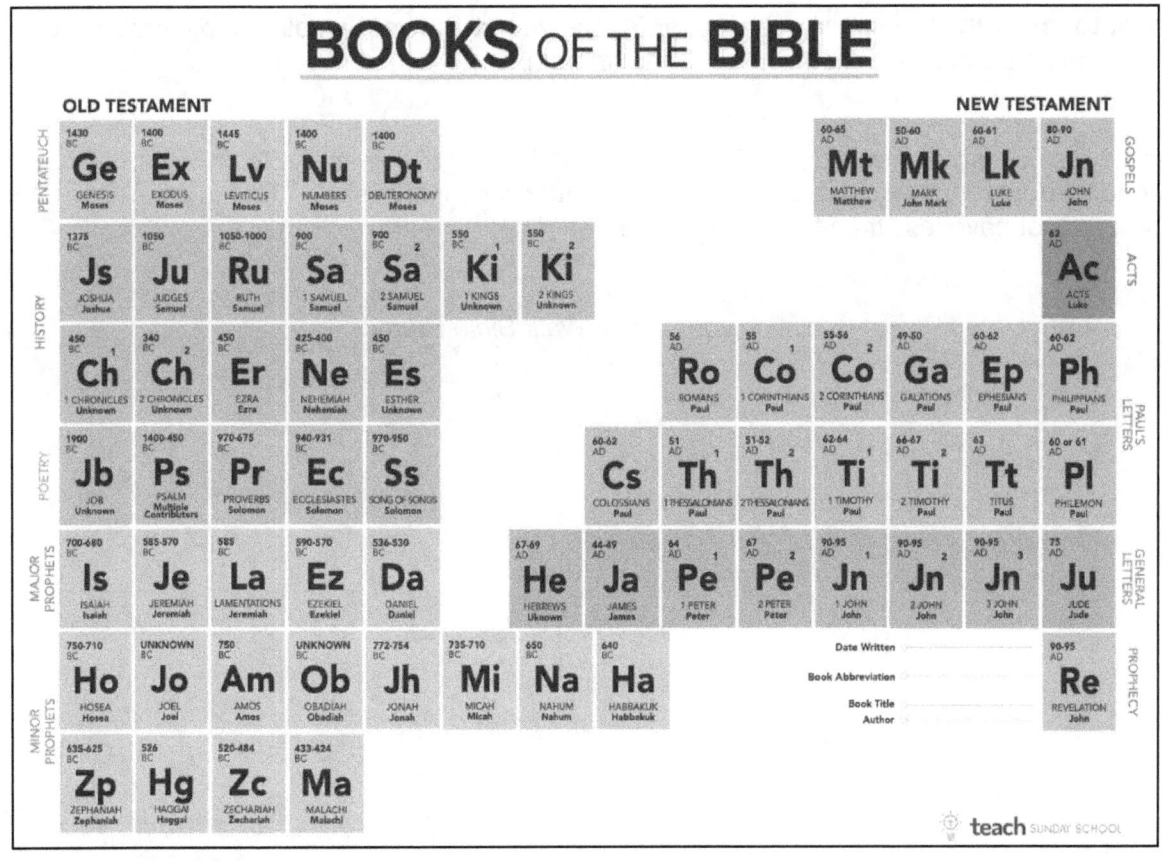

DISCUSSION GROUP GUIDELINES

Anyone can do this study alone. If you are doing this as part of a group, we suggest you use the following guidelines to maintain a safe environment for your group members to learn together.

1. **Attend consistently** whether your lesson is done or not. You will learn from the other women, and they want to get to know you.

2. **Set aside time** to work through the study questions. The goal of Bible study is to **get to know** Jesus. He will change your life.

3. **Share your insights** from your personal study time. As you spend time in the Bible, Jesus will teach you truth through His Spirit inside you.

4. **Respect each other's insights**. Listen thoughtfully. Encourage each other as you interact. Refrain from dominating the discussion if you have a tendency to be talkative. ☺

5. **Celebrate our unity** in Christ. Avoid bringing up controversial subjects such as politics, divisive issues, and denominational differences.

6. **Maintain confidentiality.** Remember that anything shared during the group time is not to leave the **group** (unless permission is granted by the one sharing).

7. **Pray for one another** as sisters in Christ.

8. **Get to know the women** in your group. Please do not use your small group members for solicitation purposes for home businesses, though.

There is a small group discussion guide available at the end of this study. Anyone can use the guide to lead a group through a discussion of the questions in this study. This is especially useful for groups that have less than two hours to meet together.

Enjoy your Joyful Walk Bible Study!

> **Recommended:** Listen to the podcast "Remember Your Identity in a Pull-Apart World" as an introduction to the whole study. Use the listener guide below.

Remember Your Identity in a Pull-Apart World

YOUR IDENTITY IS IN THE LORD

- The Jews were God's people, chosen specifically by Him to reflect His holiness and represent the true God to the unbelieving world around them. Sadly, many of the Jews forgot to remember their identity as belonging to God and not to the world.

- Christians have an identity that says, "Belonging to God." We are chosen, redeemed from the slavery to sin, adopted as God's children, and clothed with Christ's righteousness. *1 Corinthians 6:19-20*

REMEMBER THE LORD

- The word "remember" is used repeatedly throughout the Old Testament of God remembering His promises to His people and acting on them.

- God's people are called to remember who God is, what He has done for us, and who we are in God's hands. Remembering is **not passive**. It is an action that requires turning your heart to God to listen to Him and to obey Him.

- Remembering means that you choose not to forget. *Psalm 103:2-5; 77:10-14*

- You must remember who God is, His sovereignty, His love, and His grace toward you embodied in Jesus Christ. *Isaiah 46:8-10; 1 Corinthians 11:23-25*

- When you remember the power of God and His promises to you, you are set free to stop focusing on the "impossible" and focus on the God who **does the impossible**.

RECOMMIT YOUR HEART TO THE LORD

- In the Bible, "recommit" is related to repentance and returning to the Lord. You need to recommit to Him whenever you have been negligent. You need to recommit to Him whenever you are facing challenges that tempt you to follow the world's way or your own way instead of God's way. *1 Kings 8:61*

- A committed heart is at rest because you have chosen to be devoted to God, to listen to Him, and to obey Him. Being committed to God will help you to stick to your faith in our pull-apart world.

STICKING TO YOUR FAITH

- The pull-apart culture around you continually tempts you to follow its way of doing life. Or it lures you into following your own way of doing life without any regard to God or anyone else having authority over you.

- Sticking to your faith is an ongoing, intentional action. You cannot be passive about this.

- Many Christians today live more like the world than like Christ. They are your neighbors, co-workers, friends, and family members. Pray for them to recommit themselves to God and to live life His way instead of the world's way or their own way. *Psalm 37:1-6*

- Committing your way and trusting in the Lord is sticking to your faith.

THE REWARDS FOR STICKY FAITH

- A restored relationship starts with asking God to repair and to refresh your relationship with Him. *Lamentations 5:21*

- Remembering God and His love for you and recommitting to His way of doing life will lead to restoring any missing communion with the Lord.

- The Apostle Peter wrote to Christians who were being pulled away from God by the destructive influences of their world.

  *And **the God of all grace**, who called you to his eternal glory in Christ, after you have suffered a little while, **will himself restore you, and make you strong, firm and steadfast**. To him be the power for ever and ever. Amen. (1 Peter 5:10-11)*

- This world is hostile to God and to everyone who aligns herself with God. That is a fact. But God has your back. You can trust Him. The God of all grace, who knows you, who has called you through Christ, will restore you and make you able to stick firmly to Him in the midst of a pull-apart world.

- In the Old Testament, God sent prophets, priests, and leaders to help His people remember who they were and His goodness toward them.

FOR YOU TO REMEMBER

- Christian, **remember** who you are and the wonderful things God has done for you through your faith in His Son Jesus Christ. If you have been pulled away from God by the world's destructive influences, recommit to doing life God's way rather than the world's way or your own way. Stick to your faith. And enjoy the blessings of belonging to God and living obediently to Him.

- What do you need to remember about God, His goodness to you, and your identity in Him? In what areas of life have you been pulled apart from God by the destructive influences of the world? Are you willing to trust Him and follow His way of living your life?

Let Jesus satisfy your heart with complete trust in Him so that you will follow His way of living life instead of the world's way or your own way.

Lesson 1: Jeremiah and Ezekiel to the Exiles

605-586 B.C.

DAY ONE STUDY

Ask the Lord Jesus to teach you through His Word.

Why Study the Old Testament?

Have you heard other Christians say that the Old Testament is irrelevant to us today because it was about the Jews and the old covenant they had with God (the Mosaic Law)? Yet, the New Testament writers continually quote the Old Testament, especially referring to God's promises to those who believe in Him and trust Him. The assumption is that you know the context of those quoted verses and why they are important.

New and young Christians need to focus their Bible reading and study on the New Testament. They need to know Jesus through the gospels and all that they have in Christ through Acts and the letters that follow. But once someone is established in her faith in Christ, she needs to be able to read and understand the Old Testament because God has purpose for us in those writings. Let us examine His use of the Old Testament writings in our lives today.

1. Read Romans 15:4. What purposes do "everything written in the past" (the Old Testament) have for us?

2. Read 1 Corinthians 10:6-13. What can we learn from the examples given in the Old Testament?

3. Read 2 Timothy 3:15-17. What do you learn about the Old Testament scriptures?

> **From the Greek:** "All Scripture," is divinely "inspired" (Gr. theopneustos, lit. "God-breathed," as in 2 Pet. 1:21). It does not merely contain the Word of God, or become the Word of God under certain conditions. It is God's Word, the expression of His Person (heart, mind, will, etc.). This was the view of the Hebrew Bible that Jews in the first century commonly held. (*Dr. Constable's Notes on 2 Timothy 2023 Edition*, p. 49)

4. Read 2 Peter 1:19-21. What confidence do you have when you read and study the Old Testament scriptures?

Simple Things to Know When Studying the Old Testament

The books of the Old Testament (except for Genesis and Job) are the accounts of people living under the Old Covenant, the Law of Moses. It is important to keep that background and context in mind when studying them. So here are some simple things to know when studying the Old Testament.

DIFFERENT MEANINGS FOR SOME WORDS AND PHRASES

For example:

- "Salvation" (especially in the Psalms) usually refers to a temporal *deliverance* from trouble or danger. It does not usually refer to eternal life.

- "Judge" usually refers to God or God's representative acting as a hero to defend justice and the cause of the poor and defenseless. It does not usually refer to a courtroom.

- "The Holy Spirit" empowered certain individuals *temporarily* for special service (such as artisans, prophets, or kings). The Spirit then left when that service was completed.

- "Forgiveness of sins" under the Law was accomplished through *atonement*, which means a "covering" for sin. A gracious God offered forgiveness to those who trusted in His lovingkindness, but it was at best *temporary* and *up-to-date*. The sacrifices in the Law of Moses did not provide someone forgiveness for tomorrow's sins.

SALVATION BY FAITH IN THE OLD TESTAMENT

In the Old Testament, God's grace accepted any person who came to Him by faith. They received eternal salvation by their faith alone as in the New Testament. God's method of *managing* His people, however, was different, so *how* one's faith was expressed and lived out differed as well. The Tabernacle and the temple represented the presence of God dwelling among His chosen people, Israel. There, the priests represented the people to God, and sacrificial offerings were the prime way to publicly express worship, repentance, and thanksgiving. God wanted the worshiper's *heart* first. Where one's *heart* was right, sacrifices could be acceptable to God as an expression of inner faith. While we no longer express worship to God through animal sacrifices, He still desires the hearts of His people above all else.

When Jesus Christ died on the cross, He brought to a close the age of the Old Covenant, the Law of Moses. He simultaneously inaugurated the New Covenant in which we live. Salvation is obtained by faith in Christ and His finished work on the cross. Every believer receives forgiveness for all sin—past, present, and future. Salvation is also secure and never taken away. New Testament believers have a permanent indwelling of the Holy Spirit who gives us eternal life and His daily empowering presence. God continues to deliver His people from some things but not all dangers as He uses some challenges to teach us to rely on Him more than on ourselves.

"DESCRIPTIVE" VERSUS "PRESCRIPTIVE" IN THE NARRATIVES

Much of the Old Testament is written in narrative form. For example, Genesis through Esther are mostly historical books. Yet, even parts of the books of prophecy are narrative (as in Jeremiah, Ezekiel, and Daniel). Narrative means the text describes what happened. It is descriptive, not usually prescriptive—a very important difference.

- **Descriptive** means the observation of what actually happened, how people lived and made choices on how to do life at the time. For example, *"David and all the Israelites were celebrating with all their might before God, with songs and with harps, lyres, timbrels, cymbals and trumpets"* (1 Chronicles 13:8). This is not a restriction on the types of instruments that can be used in worship.

- **Prescriptive** means a command from God about how to live or do something that applies to all believers, all people groups, and all time periods. For example, *"Love the Lord your God with all your heart and with all your soul and with all your strength"* (Deuteronomy 6:5). This applies to every human who is alive or has ever lived.

Unless it is prescriptive, you cannot take passages from Old Testament narratives and create a formula for doing things a certain way to guarantee God's blessing on the result.

READ FOR ACCURACY THEN APPLY NEW TESTAMENT TRUTH

As you study Old Testament books, read first to obtain accurate understanding of what the author(s) meant. Then, use New Testament teachings to apply truth about God to your everyday life in Jesus Christ. That is what we will be doing in this study. Each lesson will help you understand what the author's original intent was based on language studies and translation comparisons plus any historical information about the time period. Then, you are directed to consider what is taught in the New Testament about our life with Christ that applies to current situations similar to what is found in the Old Testament passages you study.

5. What grabbed your attention from "Simple Things to Know When Studying the Old Testament?"

Historical Background for This "Identity" Study

From Genesis, we learn that the Jewish people descended from a man named Abraham. God called Abraham out of his home country (Ur of the Chaldeans that ironically became part of Babylon later) and sent him to Canaan (modern Israel). God promised him zillions of descendants, a specific area of land, and a blessing for the whole world that would come through Him. Abraham's descendants moved to Egypt where they grew in number for ~400 years but became slaves of the Egyptian rulers. So God delivered them from bondage through Moses who took the people across the Red Sea to Mt. Sinai where God gave them their Law for daily living in His presence.

After 40 years, God led them to their promised land and helped them establish themselves there. He provided priests, prophets, and kings to help the people know God, love God, and serve God. Israel was supposed to be God's representatives to the nations of the world. But the people kept getting drawn away to the evil practices of the nations around them. The united nation under Saul, David, and Solomon split into two kingdoms: The Northern Kingdom was called Israel, and the Southern Kingdom was called Judah.

With the destruction of the Northern Kingdom by Assyria in 722 B.C., Judah remained alone. She had been able to escape an early ruin because the Davidic dynasty remained stable, and many of Judah's kings were godly (Asa, Jehoshaphat, Uzziah, Hezekiah, and Josiah). Zealous prophets exhorted Judah to love and obey God. Elijah, Elisha, Amos, and Hosea had ministered to Israel. Isaiah, Habakkuk, and Jeremiah poured out their messages of repentance and faith upon Judah.

Wicked kings, however, like Ahaz and Manasseh damaged the moral fiber of the people. The idolatrous worship of foreign gods (Baal and Molech especially) remained a temptation. Judah had stayed strong until the reign of Manasseh, whose destructive influence so undermined the nation (Jeremiah 15:2-4) that not even his godly grandson Josiah could rescue her from the downward slide. With the death of Josiah in 609 B.C., Judah's end came quickly.

After about 700 years of living in their promised land, God determined that the Jewish people would be in a "70-year time out" from living in their land because of their evil behavior. The writer of 2 Chronicles 36:15-21 summarized what happened that led to this drastic measure taken by a loving God.

> ***The Lord, the God of their ancestors, sent word to them*** *through his messengers again and again, because **he had pity on his people** and on his dwelling place. But they mocked God's messengers, despised his words and scoffed at his prophets until the wrath of the Lord was aroused against his people and **there was no remedy**. He brought up against them the king of the Babylonians, who killed their young men with the sword in the sanctuary, and did not spare young men or young women, the elderly or the infirm. God gave them all into the hands of Nebuchadnezzar. He carried to Babylon all the articles from the temple of God, both large and small, and the treasures of the Lord's temple and the treasures of the king and his officials. They set fire to God's temple and broke down the wall of Jerusalem; they burned all the palaces and destroyed everything of value there. He carried into **exile to Babylon the remnant**, who escaped from the sword, and they became servants to him and his successors until the kingdom of Persia came to power. The land enjoyed its sabbath rests; all the time of its desolation it rested, until the seventy years were completed in fulfillment of the word of the Lord spoken by Jeremiah. (2 Chronicles 36:15-21)*

Beginning in 605 B.C. and lasting about 20 years, Nebuchadnezzar made three incursions into Judah. Each time, he removed Jews from their homeland and took them into captivity in Babylon (modern Iraq) and into other areas of the Babylonian Empire (including modern Turkey and Iran). The total destruction of Jerusalem including the temple and the palace took place in 586 B.C. In Babylon, the exiled Judeans were treated with some measure of respect. For seventy years, they learned how to live in a pagan environment away from their temple and their land. Some became prosperous businessmen. Some rose to political power (Daniel and his friends). The prophets Jeremiah and Ezekiel delivered messages of hope for Israel's return according to God's promise.

After the 70 years of exile were over, the Persian king Cyrus the Great allowed the Jewish people to return to Judea and rebuild their temple in Jerusalem. Three groups of people returned over the next 100 years bringing thousands of dispersed Jews back to their homeland. This remnant of

Jews returned to a ruined Jerusalem and other obstacles to their success. Many of them who had been born in Babylon had little concept of living in the "promised land" and how to worship God there. So God in His goodness inspired someone to chronicle the history of His people from their first calling through Abraham to what happened that caused the death of the nation and exile to Babylon (1 and 2 Chronicles).

God also kept His promise to David to maintain one of David's descendants as leader of the Jews. Josiah's grandson Jehoiachin was on Judah's throne when he was carried off to Babylon as a prisoner during the second deportation of Jews in 597 B.C. along with his wives and prominent people of the land (2 Kings 24:15). Jehoiachin was later released from prison (2 Kings 25:27-30).

While in Babylon, Jehoiachin had several sons, one of whom was Shealtiel—the heir to the throne. Over time, Shealtiel's nephew Zerubbabel became the next heir to David's throne. Zerubbabel returned to Jerusalem with the exiles. He served as governor of the province of Judah but never became king. In fact, the next Davidic king to inherit the throne is Jesus Christ.

Most of the above is covered in the *Reboot Renew Rejoice Bible Study* of 1 and 2 Chronicles. *Identity: Sticking to Your Faith in a Pull-Apart World Bible Study* picks up with the Babylonian exile and continues through the resettling of the people of Israel back in their homeland. As they returned, God wanted His people to remember who they were and His goodness to them and choose to live life God's way rather than the world's way or their own way

6. What grabbed your attention from the above historical information?

7. Questions to consider as you begin this study:

   - What do you need to remember about God, His goodness to you, and your identity in Him?

   - In what areas of life have you been pulled apart from God by the destructive influences of the world?

   - Are you willing to trust Him and follow His way of living your life?

Ask the Lord Jesus to give you the strength to say "No" to those destructive influences and to stick firmly to your faith in Him.

DAY TWO STUDY

ABC's of Jeremiah

Author

Jeremiah was a prophet who came from a priestly family. Prophets could represent any of the tribes. Priests, however, only came from the tribe of Levi and specifically had to be a descendant of Aaron, Moses' brother. God determined that Jeremiah would be a prophet before Jeremiah was even born (Jeremiah 1:4-5). Jeremiah also wrote the book of Lamentations.

Background

Jeremiah faithfully served as a speaking and writing prophet for 40 years, from the time of King Josiah (620 B.C.) until after King Zedekiah's reign when the people of Jerusalem went into exile (586 B.C.). Jeremiah was often brutally treated by Israel's leaders, yet kept speaking the Lord's word to those same people.

Jeremiah experienced all three events of Jews being taken captive to Babylon. His writing addressed those living Jerusalem and Judea as well as those in exile. He experienced the fall of Jerusalem and the chaos that accompanied it.

When Nebuchadnezzar captured Jerusalem, he gave orders to take good care of Jeremiah—to free him and to give him provisions and a present (Jeremiah 39:11-40:6). He settled into his home town but was then forcibly taken to Egypt with some rebellious Jews. Jeremiah died in Egypt, being more than 70 years old.

Jeremiah 39-45 covers the fall of Jerusalem and his transport to Egypt. Daniel had access to the book of Jeremiah in Babylon (Daniel 9:2).

Context

Jeremiah, Ezekiel, and Daniel were prophets of God during the 70 years of exile. They are three of the "Major Prophets" in our Old Testament following Isaiah whose ministry occurred 100 years earlier. God's words to the Jews through Jeremiah and Ezekiel included not only what would happen to them but encouragement for how to return to trusting God and flourish while in exile.

Ask the Lord Jesus to teach you through His Word.

Read Jeremiah 24:1-10.

8. God chose the remnant of Jews who would go to Babylon. What did He promise about them in vv. 4-7?

The Chosen Remnant (The Good Figs)

Read Jeremiah 29:1-14 below.

¹ This is the text of the letter that the prophet Jeremiah sent from Jerusalem to the surviving elders among the exiles and to the priests, the prophets and all the other people Nebuchadnezzar had carried into exile from Jerusalem to Babylon. … ⁴ This is what the Lord Almighty, the God of Israel, says to all those I carried into exile from Jerusalem to Babylon: ⁵ "Build houses and settle down; plant gardens and eat what they produce. ⁶ Marry and have sons and daughters; find wives for your sons and give your daughters in marriage, so that they too may have sons and daughters. Increase in number there; do not decrease. ⁷ Also, seek the peace and prosperity of the city to which I have carried you into exile. Pray to the Lord for it, because if it prospers, you too will prosper." ⁸ Yes, this is what the Lord Almighty, the God of Israel, says: "Do not let the prophets and diviners among you deceive you. Do not listen to the dreams you encourage them to have. ⁹ They are prophesying lies to you in my name. I have not sent them," declares the Lord.
¹⁰ This is what the Lord says: "When seventy years are completed for Babylon, I will come to you and fulfill my good promise to bring you back to this place. ¹¹ For I know the plans I have for you," declares the Lord, "plans to prosper you and not to harm you, plans to give you hope and a future. ¹² Then you will call on me and come and pray to me, and I will listen to you. ¹³ You will seek me and find me when you seek me with all your heart. ¹⁴ I will be found by you," declares the Lord, "and will bring you back from captivity. I will gather you from all the nations and places where I have banished you," declares the Lord, "and will bring you back to the place from which I carried you into exile."

This letter was written from Jerusalem to those who had been taken in exile between 605 and 597 B.C. This remnant of Jews was in Babylon by God's expressed will and in His protective hand.

9. How could the faithful Jews serve the Lord in the pagan environment (vv. 5-7)?

10. What should they not do (vv. 8-9)?

Focus on the Meaning: God had declared that the exile would last 70 years and that the people were to serve the king of Babylon. The Jewish "dreamers" were false prophets who were declaring that the Jews were not to serve the king of Babylon and that the temple treasures would be soon returned to Jerusalem (Jeremiah 27:9-17), indicating a quick return of the people to their homeland. Deuteronomy 13:1-5 declares that any prophecy that did not stress obedience to God was not from God. God placed them in Babylon and would come for them when it was time for them to go home (Jeremiah 27:22).

11. What did God promise them about their future (vv. 10-11, 14)?

12. When would He fulfill that promise (v. 10)?

13. What did He want them to learn through this banishment (vv. 12-13)

14. Looking at the whole passage, what could the faithful Jews do to prepare themselves for the return to their land? See also Jeremiah 51:50.

This is what the Lord says: "Let not the wise boast of their wisdom or the strong boast of their strength or the rich boast of their riches, but let the one who boasts boast about this: that they have the understanding to know me, that I am the Lord, who exercises kindness, justice and righteousness on earth, for in these I delight," declares the Lord. (Jeremiah 9:23-24)

Additional Reading (Optional): Read Jeremiah 27-31 for the context around the passage you just studied.

The Rejected Ones (The Bad Figs)

Nebuchadnezzar appointed a Jew named Gedaliah to be the new governor of the people he left behind in Judah (2 Kings 25:22-26). Gedaliah was a descendant of Josiah's secretary of state (2 Kings 22:3). He was a friend of Jeremiah (Jeremiah 39:14) who followed that prophet's advice to cooperate with the Babylonians and stay in the land (Jeremiah 42:1-22). Gedaliah promised the remaining Israelites that if they would settle down in the land and serve the king of Babylon, things would go well with them. Yet some of those who had royal blood assassinated Gedaliah. Fearing what the Babylonians might do to them, a large group of the remaining Jews fled to Egypt, forcibly taking Jeremiah with them (Jeremiah 43:1-13). Jeremiah continued to warn those Jews in Egypt to return to God, but they refused to listen.

Read Jeremiah 7:16-19 and 44:15-29.

15. How did the unfaithful Jews continue their unfaithfulness in Egypt?

16. What choices did the women intentionally make?

17. What did God do or say through Jeremiah to encourage them to trust Him and follow His way instead of the world's way or their own way?

18. What did they need to remember about God and His actions?

19. What would be the consequences of their continued unfaithfulness in Egypt (vv. 14, 27-29)?

> **Additional Reading (Optional):** Read Jeremiah 40-44 for the context around the passage you just studied.

Application for today

Part of application is correlating events and actions in the past with similar situations today then finding New Testament verses that apply to that similar situation. That is what we will do in the chart below.

20. Consider anything in this lesson that is similar to today. Find New Testament verses that you can apply in your life to that similar situation.

> *Similar situation: Women doing what they want in rebellion against God. NT Verses: Galatians 5:20—Idolatry is sin. Watch out for any attempt to glorify womanhood over God. Acts 13:50—Do not get caught up in causes that are more self-driven than God-driven.*

Your favorite verse(s) from today's study:

Respond to the Lord about what you learned today.

DAY THREE STUDY

ABC's of Ezekiel

Author

Like Jeremiah, Ezekiel was also from a priestly family. He was among the Jews exiled to Babylon by Nebuchadnezzar in 597 B.C. While there, he received his call to become a prophet. He was married, lived in his own house, and had a relatively free existence. God used him to deliver messages to his fellow exiles, sometimes acting them out rather than speaking them. Ezekiel faithfully did what God asked him to do. His writing covers 20 years during the exile (593-573 B.C.).

Background

Both Jeremiah and Ezekiel spoke and wrote during the time period in which Jews were deported to Babylon. God's words through them included not only what would happen to them but encouragement for how to return to trusting God and flourish while living in exile.

Ezekiel was Daniel's contemporary in Babylon. But Ezekiel lived and ministered among the exiles in their settlements whereas Daniel served primarily the Gentile Babylonians and Medo-Persians in their capitals.

Context

The book of Ezekiel follows the books of Jeremiah and Lamentations in the Old Testament. These three along with Isaiah and Daniel compose what is called the "Major Prophets" section. Isaiah was written 100 years earlier. Daniel was written during and after the time of Ezekiel.

Ask the Lord Jesus to teach you through His Word.

> ***Additional Reading (Optional):*** Read Ezekiel 1:1-2:8 for the vision of God's glory and Ezekiel's calling to be a prophet to the exiles in Babylon at the age of 30.

Read Ezekiel 11:1, 16-25. Verses 22-23 are a continuation of Chapter 10.

21. What was challenging God's people?

22. What choices did they make or need to make?

23. What did God do or say to encourage them to trust Him and follow His way instead of the world's way or their own way?

Their response is not recorded for us here. During the years of captivity, many of the people changed and returned to the Lord. Ezekiel responded to the Lord by telling the exiles everything to the Lord had shown him (v. 25).

Read Ezekiel 12:15-16.

24. What was God's purpose for scattering His people?

Focus on the Meaning: The phrase "Then they will know that I am the Lord" is used sixty-five times in Ezekiel's book. God used the events of Ezekiel's life to teach His people and us today that He is the only true God. He is the only one worthy of worship and following.

Read Ezekiel 13:17-23.

Not only were the women who escaped to Egypt continuing in their unfaithfulness to God, so were some who had been taken to Babylon.

25. What was challenging God's people?

Focus on the Meaning: Once again, the women false prophets were concocting their own messages and passing them off as divine revelations. They were acting like witches and magicians, exercising power of the people. They were not encouraging obedience to God.

26. What choices did they make or need to make?

27. What did God do or say to encourage them to trust Him and follow His way instead of the world's way or their own way?

Their response is not recorded for us. But we know God would do what He said He would do. There is no further mention of them with those who returned to Jerusalem at the end of the exile.

Application for today

28. Consider anything in this lesson that is similar to today. Find New Testament verses that you can apply in your life to that similar situation.

Your favorite verse(s) from today's study:

Respond to the Lord about what you learned today.

DAY FOUR STUDY

God made special promises to His people through Jeremiah and Ezekiel that have been fulfilled by Christ's death and resurrection so they apply to us today.

Ask the Lord Jesus to teach you through His Word.

Read Jeremiah 31:31-34.

29. What did God promise to His people?

Read Ezekiel 36:24-27.

30. What did God promise to His people?

Application for today

31. Find New Testament verses relating to God's promise of the New Covenant being fulfilled.

Think About It: Read the words in the song below. They fit beautifully with our study and what God wants for us as we live in our pull-part world. You can easily find an audio version online.

> Give me one pure and holy passion, give me one magnificent obsession
> Give me one glorious ambition for my life to know and follow hard after You.
> To know and follow hard after You, to grow as Your disciple in Your truth
> This world is empty, pale, and poor Compared to knowing you my Lord
> Oh lead me on, I will run after You ("Give Me One Pure and Holy Passion," Mark Altrogge)

Respond to the Lord about what you learned today.

Recommended: Listen to the podcast "The Two Aspects of Trusting God" to reinforce what you have learned. Use the listener guide on the next page.

The Two Aspects of Trusting God

WHAT DOES IT MEAN TO TRUST GOD?

Trust = assured reliance on the character, ability, strength, or truth of someone or something (Merriam-Webster dictionary)

- When you trust God, you believe that what God says and does is true, and you are confident that you can depend upon Him.

- Trusting God is an outworking of faith. For Christians, faith is a full commitment to Christ. God acted. We respond to His action by saying yes to faith in Jesus Christ and jumping into the new life God has for us. Instead of believing in your own ability to earn God's favor, you now trust in what Christ has done for you. That is biblical faith.

- As you live your life in Christ, you choose to trust Him daily for whatever it is you are called to do.

TWO ASPECTS OF TRUSTING GOD

- Has God placed something in your heart for you to do for Him? Or has He placed you in a situation where you need to act on His behalf?

- Whatever it is involves two aspects of trusting God. It is like having two interlocking pieces that fit together to make a whole. What are those two pieces to trusting God?

  - ✓ **First piece:** You must trust Him as you do your part His way.
  - ✓ **Second piece:** You must trust Him to do His part in the areas over which you have no control. This involves trusting His goodness in whatever He chooses to do alongside what you are doing.

DOING YOUR PART GOD'S WAY

- God sent a letter through the prophet Jeremiah to all the people Nebuchadnezzar had carried into exile from Jerusalem to Babylon. God told them how to flourish during their exile. *Jeremiah 29:5-7*

- Be productive and content. Live normal lives and be fruitful. Flourish. Be useful to the city and area in which you live. Ask God to prosper it. That is doing your part God's way.

- Doing your part God's way also applies to discernment about any teaching you hear. *Jeremiah 29:8-9*

- There are always deceivers among us who like to gain control over an audience through anything sensational. That is true for dreams, visions, and prophecies.

- We as believers in God need to be discerning about what we read and hear. That means we need to know the truth of God's word. Then, we can test what someone is teaching against the truth that we know.

Anything that does not exalt Christ as Lord of your life over anything else is not from God.

- Beware of the causes you support and watch out for any attempt to glorify anything over the Lord Jesus. *Jeremiah 44:15-19*

TRUSTING GOD TO DO HIS PART

- While you are living life God's way, flourishing as He wants you to flourish in whatever situation you find yourself, you must trust God to do His part in whatever He chooses to do. That might require a long wait in your current challenging situation. *Jeremiah 29:10-14*

- God was working in the background to carry out His plans for them. They had to wait seventy years to go home, though. And during that seventy years, their hearts would become softer toward God. They would want Him so much that they would seek Him with all their heart.

- God knew the time they spent in exile would prepare them for a future back in their homeland. It would take seventy years of cleansing their hearts and minds from all the pollution of idolatry that had infiltrated their lives. God promised to bring those in Babylon back to their land and also those who had been carried away into other countries. He was watching over them all and knew where every Israelite was. He also knew whose hearts would be turned toward Him. Those would be the ones He would bring home. *Ezekiel 11: 17-20*

- The Jews in Babylon did flourish. They were given fertile land on which to farm. They lived in their own houses and built businesses. Artefacts record how they were renting, buying, and selling. They enjoyed freedom of movement and maintained their Jewish society, with their elders governing them. Yet, they knew it was still a punishment for their idolatrous behavior. They had to trust God to do His part while they were doing their part His way. That is what we need to do as well.

- The result of the two aspects of trusting God is that you will want to follow His way of living life instead of the world's way or your own way. Trust leads to obedience and peace. Trust leads to flourishing.

Let Jesus satisfy your heart with complete trust in Him so that you will follow His way of living life instead of the world's way or your own way.

Lesson 2: Daniel 1-8

605-538 B.C.

DAY ONE STUDY

ABCs of Daniel

Author

When Nebuchadnezzar invaded Judah in 605 B.C., he took some royal and noble captives to Babylon including Daniel and his friends. This action had been predicted by the prophet Isaiah 100 years earlier (Isaiah 39:5-7). The travel time from Jerusalem to Babylon lasted about 4 months. Daniel was probably a young teenager (13-14) when he arrived in Babylon, based on the Hebrew words used to describe him. He was "enrolled" in a three-year indoctrination school along with his three Hebrew friends. Then, he was taken into Nebuchadnezzar's service. He stayed in government service for about 70 years.

Background

> In 605 B.C., Prince Nebuchadnezzar led the Babylonian army of his father Nabopolassar against the allied forces of Assyria and Egypt. He defeated them at Carchemish, which was then under Assyrian control. This victory gave Babylon supremacy in the ancient Near East. With Babylon's victory, Egypt's vassals, including Judah, passed under Babylonian control. Shortly thereafter that same year Nabopolassar died, and Nebuchadnezzar succeeded him as king. Nebuchadnezzar then moved south and invaded Judah, also in 605 B.C. He took some royal and noble captives to Babylon, including Daniel, plus some of the vessels from Solomon's temple (2 Chron. 36:7). This was the first of Judah's three deportations in which the Babylonians took groups of Judahites to Babylon. ... in 597 B.C., [Nebuchadnezzar] took [Israel's king] Jehoiachin to Babylon, along with most of Judah's remaining leaders, including young Ezekiel, and the rest of Judah's national treasures (2 Kings 24:10-17; 2 Chron. 36:10). A third and final deportation took place approximately 11 years later, in 586 B.C. After an 18-month siege, Jerusalem fell. Nebuchadnezzar returned to Jerusalem, burned the temple, broke down the city walls, and took all but the poorest of the Jews captive to Babylon. (*Dr. Constable's Notes on Daniel 2022 Edition*, pp. 1-2)

By the time Ezekiel arrived in Babylon, Daniel had been there for seven years. Ezekiel lived and ministered among the Israelites. In contrast, Daniel lived and worked primarily among Gentiles. He served in advisory and administrative roles in the government of the Babylonian kings. His book is composed of both historical narratives telling what was happening (chapters 1-7) and apocalyptic literature revealing future events in the plan of God (chapters 8-12). Daniel is one of three Old Testament books that is apocalyptic. The other two books are Ezekiel (37:1-14; 40:1-48:35) and Zechariah (chapters 9-14).

Context

The Jews placed this book in the Writings section of their Scriptures because Daniel was not a typical Hebrew prophet. He spoke God's words to kings as a prophet did and wrote inspired Scripture. But he was a government official in a Gentile land rather than a preaching prophet. The translators of the Hebrew Old Testament into Greek (the Septuagint) placed the book of Daniel among the other Major Prophets (Isaiah, Jeremiah, Lamentations, and Ezekiel) because of its prophetic content. The Latin translators did the same. So our English versions place Daniel as the last book in the Major Prophets section of the Old Testament, coming just before the 12 Minor Prophets. Haggai, Zechariah, and Malachi follow Daniel chronologically as prophets. The books Ezra, Nehemiah, Esther, and Chronicles follow Daniel historically. The book of Daniel covers all 70 years of the exile before the return of the Jews to their homeland. It clearly shows how God orchestrates history, including kings and kingdoms, to fulfill His ultimate will for human history. This is seen especially in Daniel chapters 2, 5, and 7-9. As you will see, the book of Daniel is more about the God of Daniel than it is about Daniel himself.

See the maps of the Babylonian and Persian Empires in the back of this book.

Ask the Lord Jesus to teach you through His Word.

Read Daniel chapter 1.

Daniel, Hananiah, Mishael, and Azariah were born during the reign of the godly King Josiah who spent years getting rid of the idolatry in Jerusalem and Judah. Josiah called the people together, read the Mosaic Law in their presence, and led the people in renewing their covenant with the Lord. The parents of these boys would have been part of this covenant renewal. The Scripture says that as long as Josiah lived, the people did not fail to follow the Lord (2 Chronicles 34:29-33). Josiah died in 609 B.C., just 4 years before Nebuchadnezzar took Daniel and his friends to Babylon.

1. What was challenging Daniel, Hananiah, Mishael, and Azariah? Consider all that they had experienced.

Focus on the Meaning: The Jewish law commanded for animals to be killed in a certain way that was not the practice of the Gentile nations. Also, the choice meat and wine would likely have been presented to idols before being served at the king's table. See Acts 15:19-21 for a similar situation. God performed a miracle in keeping the boys healthy during the test. Within a short time, captive Jewish priests could be made available to prepare meat the proper way for Daniel and the others to add to their diets. Both Jeremiah and Ezekiel refer to priests present among the captives in Babylon (see Lesson One).

2. What choices did they make or need to make?

Dependent Living: There are **two aspects of trusting God**. #1-You trust God as you do your part His way (Daniel in verse 8). #2-You trust God to do His part alongside what you are doing (God in verse 9). Look for these two aspects of trusting God throughout this study.

3. What did God do or say to encourage them to trust Him and follow His way instead of the world's way or their own way?

4. How did they respond?

Historical Insight: Daniel ... continued in office as a public servant at least until 538 B.C. (1:21), and as a prophet at least until 536 B.C. (10:1). Thus the record of his ministry spans 70 years, the entire duration of the Babylonian Captivity. He probably lived to be at least 85 years old and perhaps older. ... Ezekiel mentioned Daniel (Ezek. 14:14; 28:3). Also, the Lord Jesus Christ spoke of this book as the writing of Daniel (Matt. 24:15; Mark 13:14). The Jews believed that Daniel was its writer from its earliest appearance. (*Dr. Constable's Notes on Daniel 2022 Edition*, pp. 2-3)

Application for today

5. Consider anything in this lesson that is similar to today. Find New Testament verses that you can apply in your life to that similar situation.

Your favorite verse(s) from today's study:

Respond to the Lord about what you learned today.

DAY TWO STUDY

Ask the Lord Jesus to teach you through His Word.

Read Daniel 2:1-3, 10-16, 17-49. This happened one year later in 604 B.C. Daniel was ~15.

Optional: Using the descriptions given, fill out the chart on the next page.

> **Historical Insight:** Archeologists have uncovered actual "dream manuals" presumably used by these trained bureaucrats (the 4 classes of wise men listed in Daniel 2:2). These manuals listed various images then related what each must mean. Being able to do this gave them power to influence young King Nebuchadnezzar and direct the empire.

6. What was challenging Daniel, Hananiah, Mishael, and Azariah (vv. 1-3, 10-13)?

7. What choices did they make or need to make (vv. 14-18)?

8. What did God do or say to encourage them to keep trusting Him and following His way instead of the world's way or their own way?

   - Verse 19-23—

   - Verses 27-30—

   - Verses 46-49—

Empire	Daniel 2 Description	Daniel 7 Description	Daniel 8 Description
Babylonian			— — — — — —
Medo-Persian			
Greece			
Roman			— — — — — —
Future			

553 B.C. Daniel is an older man (~64).

Read Daniel chapter 7. This is parallel to what is revealed in chapter 2.

Optional: Continue filling out the chart above.

> **Historical Insight:** Daniel chapters 2-7 are written in Aramaic, a language used by the Gentiles, appropriate concerns the future history of the Gentiles during "the times of the Gentiles" (Luke 21:24)—"that extended period of time in which the land given in covenant by God to Abraham and his descendants is occupied by Gentile powers and the Davidic throne is empty of any rightful heir in the Davidic line. The times of the Gentiles, beginning with Nebuchadnezzar's invasion of Jerusalem in 605 B.C., will continue till the Messiah returns. ... Chapter 7 recorded the general history of "the times of the Gentiles," from the time Nebuchadnezzar took the Jews into captivity until the Son of Man returns to the earth. Chapter 8 reveals more detail about the second (Persian) and third (Greek) kingdoms, and especially how they relate to Israel."(*Dr. Constable's Notes on Daniel 2023 Edition*, pp. 9, 152)

9. How is God's throne room described (vv. 9-10)?

10. What do you learn about Christ (vv. 13-14)? See also Matthew 26:64.

11. What do you learn from vv. 15-27 about God's purposes for the future?

Scriptural Insight: For us as believers today, we have experienced Christ's first coming and set up of His Church, of which we are a part. We can anticipate His return for believers (the Rapture described in 1 Thessalonians 4), the Great Tribulation (God's judgment on a rebellious world), and Christ's Second Coming (Daniel 7:13-14), and His Kingdom on earth (Daniel 2:44).

Additional Reading (Optional): Read Daniel chapter 8. This vision took place two years after the vision in chapter seven. This vision addresses what the Jews will experience in the next 300 years, especially under the control of the Greek Empire. Add the descriptions to the chart above and observations of your own below. We will cover this prophecy again in Lesson 11.

Respond to the Lord about what you learned today.

DAY THREE STUDY

Ask the Lord Jesus to teach you through His Word.

~593 B.C.

Read Daniel chapter 3.

12. What was challenging God's people—especially Shadrach, Meshach, and Abednego?

13. What choices did they make or need to make (vv. 13-18)?

14. What did God do or say to encourage them to keep trusting Him and following His way instead of the world's way or their own way?

15. What was the result (vv. 28-30)?

Possibly ~583 B.C. Daniel was in his mid-thirties.

The city of Babylon was a monument to the genius of Nebuchadnezzar. It was approximately 14 miles square straddling the Euphrates River. A great bridge some 660 feet long and 30 feet wide bridged the Euphrates River and connected the eastern and western halves of the city. Babylon had inner and outer walls protecting the city, rendering it safe from outside attack. Ancient historian Herodotus claimed the walls were 350 feet high and 87 feet thick. Walls also lined the river on either side and 150 gates of solid brass protected the entrances with 250 watchtowers above. The city was laid out in square blocks with beautiful houses, 3-4 stories high, lining the streets. Babylon also boasted one of the ancient world's seven wonders—the famous hanging gardens. The gardens were built on terraces and supported large trees. Nebuchadnezzar had begun an ambition building program that included canals and monuments such as his lavish palace and an 8-story temple of Bel.

Read Daniel chapter 4.

> **Historical Insight:** Historians have identified a seven-year period during the reign of Nebuchadnezzar when he engaged in no military activity (ca. 582-575 B.C.). This may be the seven years during which he was temporarily insane. If so, he may have had this dream in 583 or 582 B.C. If this is the approximate date, Nebuchadnezzar would have defeated the Egyptians ... and would have destroyed Jerusalem (in 586 B.C.) before he had this dream. In any case, he was at ease and resting in his palace when God gave him this revelation. (*Dr. Constable's Notes on Daniel 2022 Edition*, p. 86)

16. What did God do or say to encourage Nebuchadnezzar to trust Him and follow His way instead of the world's way or his own way?

17. How did Nebuchadnezzar respond?

- Verse 30—

- Verses 34-37—

18. What do you learn about God's sovereignty over kings, kingdoms, and human history?

19. What do you learn about God's grace toward a headstrong person like Nebuchadnezzar?

Application for today

20. Consider anything in this lesson that is similar to today. Find New Testament verses that you can apply in your life to that similar situation.

Your favorite verse(s) from today's study:

Respond to the Lord about what you learned today.

DAY FOUR STUDY

Ask the Lord Jesus to teach you through His Word.

539 B.C. Daniel was ~80 years old.

Read Daniel chapter 5.

21. What happened in vv. 1-12?

22. What choices did Daniel make or need to make (vv. 13-17)?

23. What did God do or say through Daniel to Belshazzar (vv. 18-28)?

24. What happened then?

> **Historical Insight**: Isaiah and Jeremiah had predicted Babylon's fall (Isa. 13:17-22; 21:1-10; 47:1-5; Jer. 51:33-58). The Persians diverted the water from the Euphrates River that flowed south through Babylon into an ancient lake located to the north. This allowed them to walk into the city on the riverbed and scale the undefended walls that flanked the river. (*Dr. Constable's Notes on Daniel 2022 Edition,* pp. 107-108)

Read Daniel chapter 6. This occurred shortly after the takeover.

> **Historical Insight:** Darius the Mede (Daniel 5:30-6:1) was not the same man as Darius the Great (Ezra 5:6, 6:1).

25. What was challenging God's people, especially Daniel (vv. 1-9)?

26. What choices did Daniel make or need to make (vv. 10-16)?

> **Think About It:** Notice the unintended consequences of Darius the Mede's rash decision. When he realized what he had done, he was very distressed. Rash decisions often lead to unintended consequences, don't they?

27. What did God do or say to encourage them to trust Him and follow His way instead of the world's way or their own way (vv. 17-23)?

28. What as the result (vv. 25-28)?

Application for today

29. Consider anything in this lesson that is similar to today. Find New Testament verses that you can apply in your life to that similar situation.

Your favorite verse(s) from today's study:

Respond to the Lord about what you learned today.

Recommended: Listen to the podcast "Daniel—Trusting God with Opposition and Dreams" to reinforce what you have learned. Use the listener guide on the next page.

Daniel—Trusting God with Opposition and Dreams

DANIEL AND HIS FRIENDS

- Daniel's family along with others were uprooted from Jerusalem and taken to Babylon as captives of King Nebuchadnezzar. Daniel and three of his friends were ripped out of those captured families and forcibly taken into a special training school for the king's service.

- Those four young men had a firm grip on their identity as belonging to the true God.

DANIEL CHAPTER 1

- Daniel took a stand on the one thing that he could—not to eat meat that had likely been prepared in a way that was against the Mosaic Law. *Daniel 1:8-9, 15*

- Daniel resolved not to defile himself. So he respectfully asked for permission that the four of them not be forced to defile themselves with that food. They did their part God's way.

- Then, they trusted God to give them favor with the official and to nourish their bodies during those ten days so that they looked healthy. God did that!

- And God rewarded their trust in Him by giving them wisdom and understanding of all that they were learning so they became useful to the king. The two aspects of trusting God.

DANIEL CHAPTER 2

- When confronted with the king's decree to kill all the wise men, Daniel stepped forth to save the lives of himself and the other wise men. *Daniel 2:14, 16-19*

- Daniel responded with wisdom and tact, asking for the facts. He spoke respectfully to the king, asked for time, and expressed that he wanted to interpret the dream for the king. He sought his three friends to join him in prayer. This is doing his part God's way.

- The four young men asked God for mercy and to reveal the mystery of the dream. God did both. Daniel praised God for doing what only He could do.

- The king was satisfied and even honored God who revealed understanding of his mysterious dream. Daniel and his friends were all promoted to higher positions in the government which gave them greater influence for God in their work.

DANIEL CHAPTER 3

- When confronted with the choice of bowing down to Nebuchadnezzar's golden statue, Daniel's three friends did not give in to the pull-apart pressure. *Daniel 3:15-18*

- The three friends chose not to bow down to a statue. They replied respectfully to the king and declared about the power and faithfulness of their God. They did their part God's way.

- They trusted God to deliver them from the king's hand either by not letting them be incinerated or taking them to their eternal home with God after death. God rescued them in such a miraculous way that the king was amazed and praised God for what He did.

- In chapter 6, Daniel trusted God by continuing his daily prayers. And he trusted God to take care of him in the lions' den however God chose to do it.

- What shines through Daniel's life is that God still does amazing things by very old people, who actually grow in usefulness over the years as they grow in their trust of God.

DANIEL AND DREAMS

- The book of Daniel is more about God than it is about Daniel. God gives favor, changes hearts of kings, answers prayer, and gives dreams plus interpretations. The temptation to put any kind of sensational interpretation to elements of dreams is paganism.

- Dreams are the continued functioning of the mind during sleep. They can reflect recent thoughts and events so that your mind creates scenarios based on fears and hopes.

- Dreams cannot be seen by another person. We cannot read minds. *Daniel 2:10-11; 26-28*

BIBLICAL TRUTH ABOUT DREAMS

1. **Dreams in which God speaks to a person are always initiated by God not that person.** In Daniel chapter 2, Daniel asked God to reveal the dream that God had already initiated to Nebuchadnezzar.

2. **Only God can reveal the meaning of any dream that He initiates.** Anything God reveals to someone in a dream will agree with what He has already revealed in His Word.

3. **Dreams from God will always encourage complete obedience to God.** Any dream, vision, or prophecy that does not stress obedience to God is **not from God**. Visions and prophecies can be self-generated.

4. **Dreams from God will never dethrone Christ from being absolute Lord of your life.** Anything that does not exalt Christ as Lord of your life over anything else is not from God.

   If you have a dream and feel that perhaps God gave it to you, prayerfully examine the Word of God and make sure your dream agrees with Scripture. If it is, prayerfully consider what God would have you do in response to your dream (James 1:5). In Scripture, whenever anyone experienced a dream from God, God always made the meaning of the dream clear, whether directly to the person, through an angel, or through another messenger. When God speaks to us, He makes sure His message is clearly understood. (gotquestions.org)

Let Jesus satisfy your heart with complete trust in Him so that you will follow His way of living life instead of the world's way or your own way.

Lesson 3: Ezra 1:1-5:2; Haggai 1-2

538-520 B.C.

DAY ONE STUDY

Author

Ezra was a priest and a teacher of the Law, also called a scribe (Ezra 7:21). This is the reference to scribes, which were prominent in the Gospels. A scribe was a student, interpreter, teacher, and preacher of the Word of God. Because of similarity of style, many believe that Ezra wrote 1 and 2 Chronicles as well as the book that bears his name. He undoubtedly had documents he could access for the historical sections in Ezra chapters 1-6. Ezra himself does not appear on the scene until chapters 7-10.

As a scribe, Ezra had the qualifications needed to write this book. He was also a contemporary of Nehemiah (Nehemiah. 8:1-9; 12:36). It is thought this book was written about 446 B.C. or shortly after that.

Background

The setting of Ezra chapters 1-6 is the postexilic era when the faithful Israelites were allowed to return from Babylon to Judah. A century before the Babylonian Exile even began, the prophet Isaiah told the people that they would experience exile, would return to their land, and the king who would allow them to return would be named Cyrus (Isaiah 44:28-45:1).

From historical records, we know that Cyrus was a great leader and administrator. As king over his ever-expanding empire, Cyrus allowed conquered people to return to their former homes, believing that this would please them and discourage rebellion. He also entrusted some responsibility of governing to native princes as we will see in the book of Ezra.

After King Cyrus of Persia's decree for the Jews to rebuild the temple in Jerusalem (Ezra 1:1-4), a group of ~50,000 Jews returned in 538 B.C. The trip took about a month, traveling 15-20 miles per day. Those who came back to their homeland included **Zerubbabel**, a grandson of King Jehoiachin (1 Chronicles 3:17-19) who was a legitimate heir to the throne of David. Zerubbabel became the governor of the reclaimed land (Ezra 3:2; Haggai 1:1). His appointment as governor allowed his Judean royal descent to coincide with his Persian political appointment. How long he served in that capacity cannot be determined, but he was still governor by 520 B.C. Zerubbabel is in the genealogy of Christ through both Joseph (Matthew 1:12-16) and Mary (Luke 3:27). Jesus was, therefore, the rightful heir to the throne of Israel.

To restore temple worship, the returning Jews needed priests and Levites. Only descendants of Aaron could serve as priests (1 Chronicles 6:48-49). **Jeshua** was the high priest of the restoration community and a descendant of Aaron. He was the son of Jehozadak, who had gone into Babylonian captivity in 586 B.C. (1 Chronicles 6:15). Joshua was apparently the grandson of Seraiah, who was the high priest Nebuchadnezzar executed when he destroyed Jerusalem (2 Kings 25:18-21; Jeremiah 52:24-27). Ezra 2:36-54 gave the names of those who could do the religious duties for the people returning, including the men and women singers (v. 64).

Ezra chapter 7 relates the arrival of Ezra who led another group of Jews returning to Israel. By then, the temple had been rebuilt in Jerusalem. Through Ezra's faithful teaching ministry, the majority of the people turned from their sinful behavior and recommitted themselves to following God's will for their lives.

Context

Ezra is one of the last three books in the historical section of the Old Testament, followed by Nehemiah and Esther. It chronologically follows the books of 2 Kings and 2 Chronicles. The genealogical lists in 1 Chronicles chapters 1-9 are connected to the return of the exiles from Babylon and the need to remember one's tribal heritage and purpose in the plan and purpose of God.

> **Historical Insight:** The earliest historical reference in Ezra is to the decree of Cyrus that he issued in his first year on the throne (1:1): 538 B.C. The latest historical reference was just prior to Nehemiah's first trip back to Jerusalem (4:21-23; cf. Neh. 1:1-3), in 446 B.C. Therefore this book spans a period of 92 years of history. However, most of the events recorded took place in 538-515 B.C. (chapters 1—6) and 458 B.C. (chapters 7—10). Between these two separate series of events the Book of Ezra records nothing. The events in the Book of Esther transpired during those years (in 482-473 B.C.). The book of Ezra and then Nehemiah record the last events, chronologically, in the Old Testament. (*Dr. Constable's Notes on Ezra 2022 Edition*, p. 6)

See the "Chronology of the Restoration Period" charts at the back of this study guide to see how Ezra fits with Haggai and Zechariah.

Ask the Lord Jesus to teach you through His Word.

538-536 B.C.

Read Ezra 1:1-8, 11.

1. What do you learn from Ezra 1:1-8, 11 about…?

- The work of God—

- The response of the people—

> **Historical Insight:** In the ancient near east, when one army defeated the other, the victors would take the images of their defeated foes captive, and lock them up, in order to testify to the impotence of those gods. Since the Israelites had no images of Yahweh, Nebuchadnezzar took the temple utensils in their place.3 Cyrus released these utensils so that the returning Jews could take them back to Jerusalem and use them in their temple worship. … There is no evidence that the Babylonians took the ark of the covenant to Babylon, or that the returning Jews brought it with them back to the Promised Land. Josephus wrote that the ark was not in the holy of holies in the second temple. (*Dr. Constable's Notes on Ezra 2022 edition*, pp. 20-21)

Read Ezra 2:1-2; 61-70.

The distance from Babylon to Jerusalem was ~900 miles, taking them four months to travel.

2. What was challenging God's people?

3. What choices did they make or need to make?

Scriptural Insight: The High priest wore a breastpiece containing twelve precious stones representing the 12 tribes. Two other stones called the Urim and the Thummim were in a pouch in the breastpiece. The Urim and Thummim were "sacred lots used as the 'means of making decisions' (Exodus 28:30). The word 'Urim' begins with the first letter of the Hebrew alphabet and 'Thummim' begins with the last letter, so the lots were probably restricted to giving either positive or negative responses to questions asked of them.
... We possess as [Christian] believers a gift in us to guide and direct our steps; it is the Holy Spirit. He is our Urim and Thummim." (*Dr. Constable's Notes on Exodus 2022 Edition,* pp. 258-259)

Read Psalm 137 (Remember).

Psalm 137 was definitely written after the people returned from the Babylonian exile. Some think that Psalm 126 was also written after the exile.

4. What do you learn from this psalm?

Read Psalm 126 (Restore).

5. What do you learn from this psalm?

Application for today

6. Consider anything in this lesson that is similar to today. Find New Testament verses that you can apply in your life to that similar situation.

7. The Jewish people had gone through difficult years of captivity and were now coming out on the other side. They could see how their God faithfully carried them through that time and were able to rejoice and even laugh again. **Read 2 Corinthians 4:7-8; 17-18.** Consider a difficult time you have been through. In what ways can you now see God was with you? Are you now able to view that time as "light and momentary affliction" in view of the eternal value that resulted from it?

Your favorite verse(s) from today's study:

Think About It: God does not discard what He has chosen, but He remakes it when it fails. (*Dr. Constable's Notes on Ezra 2022 Edition*, p. 10)

Respond to the Lord about what you learned today.

DAY TWO STUDY

Ask the Lord Jesus to teach you through His Word.

Read Ezra chapter 3.

> **Historical Insight:** "The peoples around them" (v. 3) would be those foreigners brought into the northern kingdom of Israel almost 200 hundred years earlier plus the poor people left by Nebuchadnezzar in 586 B.C. The imported people had a corrupted form of Yahweh worship blended with worshiping their own gods (2 Kings 17:24-33). The New Testament refers to them as the Samaritans. Those people who "possessed" the vacated land during the exile were not happy about the Jews returning to repossess their land and settle back into their home towns. The opposition bribed the non-Israelite officials set in place after the Babylonian conquest to work against the Jews. The decree of Cyrus made any opposition illegal, but he was hundreds of miles away. This power struggle continued through the reign of Darius I of Persia and his successors.

8. What was challenging God's people?

9. What choices did they make or need to make?

10. Whom did God give as leaders to encourage them to reestablish life God's way in Judah and Jerusalem?

11. How did the people respond?

Historical Insight: The Jews showed their earnest desire to serve and love Yahweh. They rallied around the Law of Moses and were careful to follow it. "The group that became the Pharisees (lit. Separated Ones) came into existence during the Captivity. They wanted to prevent the Jews from intermixing with others." (*Dr. Constable's Notes on Ezra 2022 Edition,* p. 10)

Read Ezra 4:1-5, 24.

Note: Ezra 4:6-23 happened 70 years later during the time of Nehemiah.

Historical Insight: Judah was surrounded by antagonistic neighbors to whom the edict of Cyrus came as a profound disappointment. In particular, the Phoenicians had been granted the coastal plain, mixed-breed Samaritans held the old Israeli lands, and Idumeans controlled south of Hebron. (Wayne Braudrick, *Nehemiah Change Agent: Catalyst* sermon, January 7, 2018)

12. What was challenging God's people?

   • Verses 1-3—

   • Verses 4-5—

13. What choices did they make or need to make?

   • Verses 1-3—

   • Verses 4-5, 24—

Focus on the Meaning: The enemies did not worship Yahweh exclusively. They had other gods. Their motives were clearly subversive as seen in verses 4-5, 24. Their "sharing" could have been to share in controlling the temple itself. After Jerusalem was destroyed, a corrupt "worship" of Yahweh had moved to Bethel. Zerubbabel realized their commitment to God did not include a commitment to obey His revealed will in the Law of Moses.

We have no record of God saying or doing anything during this time nor do we have a record of the people inquiring of God what they should do. We will see in Haggai 1:2 what became their excuse for giving up on the building of the temple.

Application for today

14. Has someone worked really hard to stop you from doing what you knew God wanted you to do? How? What did you do or should you do to overcome that?

15. Consider anything else in this lesson that is similar to today. Find New Testament verses that you can apply in your life to that similar situation.

Your favorite verse(s) from today's study:

Respond to the Lord about what you learned today.

DAY THREE STUDY

ABCs of Haggai

Author

Haggai was a Jewish prophet living among those who returned from exile to their homeland. Haggai referred to himself as simply "the prophet Haggai" (Haggai 1:1). He is unknown except for his writing and two references to him in Ezra (5:1; 6:14). We know nothing about Haggai's parents, ancestors, or tribal origin. His name apparently means "Festal" or possibly "Feast of Yahweh." This is appropriate since he spoke to the people at the time of the Jewish fall festivals. Haggai affirmed the divine authority of his messages from "the Lord Almighty" twenty-five times. He was fully aware he was God's messenger (Haggai 1:13).

Though Haggai referred to the former glory of the temple before the Babylonians destroyed it (2:3), that does not mean that he saw that temple although some in his audience definitely did.

Background

Within a year, the returnees rebuilt the altar in Jerusalem, resumed offering sacrifices on it, celebrated the Feast of Tabernacles, and laid the foundation for the reconstruction of the temple (536 B.C.). This temple is often called the second temple or Zerubbabel's temple. The work was quickly halted by protesting Samaritans and others living in the land. The zeal of the returning exiles soon settled into spiritual apathy and diversion of their energies into other areas of life—rebuilding houses, clearing land, and planting crops. Haggai and Zechariah began their ministries eighteen years after the first return of exiles to the land of Israel. In 520 B.C., God spoke to the people through Haggai during a period of 4 months—August through December. Haggai gave 4 sermons to the people during that time. The message of Haggai was effective in shaking the Jews from their lethargy.

Context

The book of Haggai is tenth in the order of the twelve Minor Prophets (Hosea–Malachi). They are "minor" only in the sense of being much shorter than the works of Isaiah and Jeremiah. In the Hebrew Bible, these writings are regarded as one book, being lumped together because they took up a scroll about the same size as that of Isaiah. Haggai is the second shortest book in the Old Testament. Obadiah is the shortest. Haggai also gave historical dating for his messages making them easy to fit into a chronological framework of Old Testament history. Haggai was the first writing prophet to address the returned Israelites. As we will see in the next lesson, Zechariah began prophesying to the returnees shortly thereafter.

One change to note in the books written after the destruction of Jerusalem, the historical references are related to the name and reign of the Gentile kings. Previously, historical references were related to the reign of a king of Judah or Israel. But the Jews had no king now. The times of the Gentiles had begun and continued through the time of Christ (Luke 1:5; 2:1).

Ask the Lord Jesus to teach you through His Word.

16 years later; 520 B.C.

Read Ezra 5:1-2 and Haggai chapter 1.

> **From the Hebrew:** Haggai, Zechariah, and Malachi referred to God almost exclusively as "the Lord Almighty," (nearly 100 times in all). This title refers to God as the Lord of armies, the highest and most absolute ruler in the whole universe, including the Persian emperor and all the administrators who serve him. They need not fear any earthly king.

16. What was challenging God's people?

17. What choices did they make or need to make?

18. What did God do or say to encourage them to trust Him and follow His way instead of the world's way or their own way?

- Verses 1-11—

- Verses 12-14—

Think About It: For 16 years, God tried to get their attention through frustrating their efforts at "prosperity." From the beginning of the Jewish people, God had a visible dwelling place among His people—the pillars of cloud and fire (Exodus 13:21-22, the tabernacle (Exodus 40:34-38; Joshua 18:1), and the temple (1 Kings 8:22-54). Then, that temple was destroyed in 586 B.C. For fifty years, the Jews had become accustomed to not having God's visible presence with them. The exiles had become content to restart their sacrifices to God and live by the Mosaic Law once again in their land. But God wanted them to want Him!

19. How did the people respond?

Application for today

20. Christians have the Holy Spirit—God's empowering presence—within us and the security of our salvation. Yet, we can be like the Jews of Haggai's day when it comes to neglecting time with God. Consider good things we can substitute for spending time with God and His Word— listening to Christian music, podcasts, and sermons; reading blogs and books; good behavior and good works; family and work responsibilities, or even just reading a daily devotional. Do you let these things satisfy your soul instead of planning for and spending time sitting in the Lord's presence, reading His Word to you, and responding back to Him in prayer and obedience?

21. Consider anything else in this lesson that is similar to today. Find New Testament verses that you can apply in your life to that similar situation.

Your favorite verse(s) from today's study:

Respond to the Lord about what you learned today.

DAY FOUR STUDY

Ask the Lord Jesus to teach you through His Word.

Read Haggai 2:1-9. This is about a month after they started the work.

Read the Bible passage below (NIV). Use your own method (colored pencils, lines, shapes) to mark anything that grabs your attention, especially God's actions or words.

> **2** *¹ on the twenty-first day of the seventh month, the word of the Lord came through the prophet Haggai: ² "Speak to Zerubbabel son of Shealtiel, governor of Judah, to Joshua son of Jozadak, the high priest, and to the remnant of the people. Ask them, ³ 'Who of you is left who saw this house in its former glory? How does it look to you now? Does it not seem to you like nothing? ⁴ But now be strong, Zerubbabel,' declares the Lord. 'Be strong, Joshua son of Jozadak, the high priest. Be strong, all you people of the land,' declares the Lord, 'and work. For I am with you,' declares the Lord Almighty. ⁵ 'This is what I covenanted with you when you came out of Egypt. And my Spirit remains among you. Do not fear.' ⁶ "This is what the Lord Almighty says: 'In a little while I will once more shake the heavens and the earth, the sea and the dry land. ⁷ I will shake all nations, and what is desired by all nations will come, and I will fill this house with glory,' says the Lord Almighty. ⁸ 'The silver is mine and the gold is mine,' declares the Lord Almighty. ⁹ 'The glory of this present house will be greater than the glory of the former house,' says the Lord Almighty. 'And in this place I will grant peace,' declares the Lord Almighty."*

22. What was challenging God's people?

23. What did God do or say to encourage them to trust Him and follow His way instead of the world's way or their own way?

Scriptural Insight: The glory of this temple exceeded Solomon's grand temple because God's own Son, Jesus Christ, was present there (Luke 2:22-35; John 12:23-32 and other times). People did come from all nations to this "house" as seen in Acts 2.

Read Haggai 2:10-23. This is 2 months later.

Scriptural Insight: Haggai 2:10-14 can be confusing to us today. Several interpretations are available. One that seems to fit is that the people thought that being back in the holy land and performing their sacrifices and offerings made them holy. Holiness comes from obeying the Lord which in this instance means to build the temple. Verses 15-17 are a reminder of what God said to them earlier (Haggai 1:5-11).

24. What did God do or say to encourage them to trust Him and follow His way instead of the world's way or their own way (verses 19-23)?

Scriptural Insight: Read Jeremiah 22:24. Haggai 2:23 is a reverse of the curse placed on Zerubbabel's grandfather Jehoiachin and guaranteed the Messianic line through Zerubbabel (Matthew 1:12-13; Luke 3:27).

The people kept working on the temple so that it was completed four years later.

Application for today

25. Consider anything in this lesson that is similar to today. Find New Testament verses that you can apply in your life to that similar situation.

Your favorite verse(s) from today's study:

Respond to the Lord about what you learned today.

> **Recommended:** Listen to the podcast "Haggai—Desiring God's Presence" to reinforce what you have learned. Use the listener guide on the next page.

Haggai—Desiring God's Presence

MOVING HOME

- The Lord **moved the heart** of King Cyrus of Persia to proclaim for all his territory that the people could go home to their land and rebuild their temple to God.

- God moved the hearts of those He wanted to go back to His land and gave them favor among their neighbors. *Ezra 1:5-6*

SETTLING BACK IN THE LAND

- Once back home, they had to learn how to live in their land again. Many of them had only lived in Babylon. They were filled with laughter and joy as they returned to their homeland. *Psalm 12:2-3*

- Have you gone through some difficult years in your life and come out on the other side with relief that it is over? Can you look back and see how God carried you through that time? Are you filled with laughter and joy because of what God has done for you?

- God provided two very capable men to lead them on this adventure—Joshua as high priest and Zerubbabel as governor of the Jews in Jerusalem and Judah. Both men were completely trusting in God to lead them and the people. What a gift to God's people!

- The first thing they did after getting settled in their homes was to build the altar to resume sacrifices. In Babylon, the Jews had not temple, so they focused on their Scriptures, especially those containing the Law. They could follow it in their dealings with one another. And they had prayer to their God. They had learned to live without sacrificing animals to God. So this new experience was a first step in restoring their worship of God. *Ezra 3:2-3*

- They began laying the foundation for the new temple. They celebrated God's faithfulness with a time of praise and worship. The sound of joy was heard far away. *Ezra 3:13*

HITTING A BRICK WALL

- The people who had been living in the land before the Jews arrived home did everything they could do to block the building. *Ezra 4:4-5, 24*

- The Jewish returnees gave in to the fear and stopped the building of their temple. They returned back to their farms and were content for the next sixteen years to bring their offerings to Jerusalem when necessary and perhaps celebrate some of their annual festivals. There is no record of them consulting God about whether to stop or not. Apparently, they took the opposition as a "No" from God and stopped. Fear and intimidation stopped their work for God and discouraged obedience to Him.

GOD SENT HAGGAI

- For sixteen years, God tried to get their attention through droughts and other hardships. They did not get the message and seek God's counsel. So God sent Haggai the prophet to make them realize their sinfulness in neglecting God. *Haggai 1:5-6*

- God wanted to be in their midst and wanted them to desire His presence with them. God's presence was represented by the temple. He placed His glory in the Holy of Holies. Did they want God's presence with them or not?

- They had gotten used to not have the temple and not needing it while living in Babylon. They had maintained their faith through following whatever part of the Law they could. Not, they could do the sacrifices again on the newly built altar. Wasn't that enough?

- God was not content to be an afterthought! He said to get to work and build His house. He said, "I am with you." They started building again within three weeks! *Haggai 1:8,14*

- God promised that His presence would be with them in that temple they were building. One day, their Messiah would enter the temple courts Himself, giving the temple they were building far greater glory than what Solomon built. *Haggai 2:7-9; John 12:23-32*

SUBSTITUTES FOR SPENDING TIME WITH GOD

- What happened to them can happen to us as believers today. We have the Spirit of God living inside of us, always with us. We have security of our salvation based upon our faith in what Christ has done for us. How can we be like them when it comes to neglecting time with our God?

- We have so many good things we can fill our time with today instead of being with God, focusing on Him, interacting with Him. We can let worship music, books, podcasts, blogs, sermon videos, and good works substitute for spending time alone with Him.

- We can do Bible studies with a focus on the information we are learning rather than interacting with our God before, during, and after each study section. That is why we prompt you to ask Jesus to teach you what He wants you to learn before each day's study and to respond to God about what you learned in that day's lesson. This is to encourage you to interact with God as you study His Word. Enjoy being in His presence.

- Our Father God wants us to desire being in His presence. When you desire Him, you will choose to spend some part of your day with Him and not all the substitutes that might make you feel good about being a Christian.

- Do God's work in your life but according to God's ways. And God's ways include interacting with Him about what His work and ways are. Desiring His presence in your life is more valuable than all the other substitutes available to us in our web-driven, social media-driven, work-driven, activity-driven, and pull-apart world.

Let Jesus satisfy your heart with complete trust in Him so that you will follow His way of living life instead of the world's way or your own way.

Lesson 4: Zechariah 1-8

520 B.C.

DAY ONE STUDY

ABCs of Zechariah

Author

Like Jeremiah and Ezekiel, Zechariah was identified as both a prophet and a priest, being the son of Berekiah and the grandson of Iddo the priest (Zechariah 1:1). His writings show that he was familiar with priestly things. He was a young man when he began prophesying (Zechariah 2:4), so he was probably born in Babylonian captivity and returned to Israel very early in life with Zerubbabel the governor and Joshua the priest (Nehemiah 12:1, 16). The name Zechariah (meaning "Yahweh Remembers") was a common one among the Israelites. At least 27 different individuals in the Old Testament were named Zechariah. It was an appropriate name for the writer of this book because Zechariah reminds the people that Yahweh (their personal name for God) remembers His chosen people and His promises to them. Their God will be faithful to them. Like the book of Daniel, there is no reason to question that Zechariah penned the entire book that carries his name.

> **Scriptural Insight**: The Lord Jesus referred to a Zechariah, the son of Berechiah, whom the Jews murdered between the temple and the altar (Matt. 23:35). This appears to be how the prophet's life ended. This would make Zechariah one of the last righteous people that the Jews killed in Old Testament history. *(Dr. Constable's Notes on Zechariah 2022 Edition, pp. 1-2)*

Background

Read the historical background for the book of Haggai in Lesson 3. Zechariah started his ministry two months after Haggai began his preaching. Zechariah continued delivering God's messages for several years afterward. In a sense, Zechariah's message complements that of Haggai. Both encourage the people to rebuild the temple so that they could enjoy God's presence with them.

Context

The ministries of Haggai and Zechariah followed those of Ezekiel and Daniel. The book of Zechariah is eleventh in the order of the twelve Minor Prophets (Hosea–Malachi). It is filled with prophecies about the Messiah. New Testament authors quoted or alluded to Zechariah's book forty-one times. The dated portions of the book (chapters 1-8) fall within the period of the rebuilding of the temple written early in his life. The undated prophecies (chapters 9-14) were likely written later in his life and focus primarily on Israel's future. Some call Zechariah the "Revelation of the Old Testament" because of its apocalyptic nature.

> **Scriptural Insight:** Our English word *apocalypse* comes from the Greek term *apokalypsis*, literally "unveiling." Apocalyptic literature in the Bible is a specific form of prophecy, largely involving symbolic imagery that is "unveiling" future grandiose, cataclysmic events in the plan of God, especially regarding the end times. The Old Testament books Ezekiel, Daniel, and Zechariah contain elements of apocalyptic literature as do certain parts of the New Testament—2 Thessalonians 2, Mark 13, Matthew 24, and the book of Revelation. The biblical apocalyptic writer had literal visions from God and faithfully

recorded them (2 Peter 1:19-21). God chose to use what we consider strange descriptions and bizarre imagery to provide clues pointing toward some future person, thing, or event in His sovereign plan for Israel, the Church, and all of humanity. God will fulfill whatever He has in mind whether we understand the symbolism or not. (adapted from *"Why is apocalyptic literature so strange?"* at gotquestions.org)

Ask the Lord Jesus to teach you through His Word.

520 B.C.

Read Ezra 5:1-2 and Zechariah chapter 1.

> **From the Hebrew:** The name for God used throughout Haggai, Zechariah, and Malachi is *Yhwh Sabaoth* (the Lord Almighty) meaning God is the supreme commander over all angelic armies plus human kings and their armies. His people can be confident in God's almighty power and His persistent purpose. He will accomplish what He has set out to do. No Persian king or any future king can stop Him.

1. From Zechariah 1:1-6, what did God do or say to encourage His people to trust Him and follow His way instead of the world's way or their own way?

2. According to Vision #1 in Zechariah 1:7-17, what did God do or say to encourage His people to trust Him and follow His way instead of the world's way or their own way?

In Vision #2 (Zechariah 1:18-20), God promised to destroy the nations that have destroyed Israel. He fulfilled that promise as Babylon overtook Assyria and Persia overtook Babylon.

Read Zechariah chapter 2.

3. According to Vision #3 in Zechariah 2:1-13, what did God do or say to encourage His people to trust Him and follow His way instead of the world's way or their own way?

    *   Verses 4-8—

    *   Verses 10-13—

Application for today

4. What do you learn about God in this lesson that encourages you today?

Your favorite verse(s) from today's study:

Respond to the Lord about what you learned today.

DAY TWO STUDY

Ask the Lord Jesus to teach you through His Word.

Read Zechariah chapter 3.

> **Scriptural Insight:** Who is the "angel of the Lord?" The precise identity is not given in the Bible. ... It seems when the definite article "the" is used, it is specifying a unique being, separate from the other angels. The angel of the Lord speaks as God, identifies Himself with God, and exercises the responsibilities of God ... Those who saw the angel of the Lord feared for their lives because they had "seen the Lord." Therefore, it is clear that in at least some instances, the angel of the Lord is a theophany, an appearance of God in physical form. Since in Zechariah 3:1-10 and 6:9-15, the angel of the Lord is present with the Lord Almighty (*Yhwh*, who is God the Father), it is possible that these appearances of the angel of the Lord were manifestations of Jesus before His incarnation (God the Son). The appearances of the angel of the Lord cease after the incarnation of Christ. (adapted from *"Who is the angel of the Lord?"* at gotquestions.org.)

Joshua (the same as "Jeshua" in Ezra 2:2 and Nehemiah 7:7) was born in Babylon. He had to learn how to be the high priest according to the Law of Moses once the temple was built. The high priest represented the people before God and God to the people. The Law of Moses said that once a year, on "Yom Kippur" (the Day of Atonement), the high priest must bathe then offer sacrifices to cleanse himself and the whole nation of sin. He then brought the blood of those sacrifices into the Holy of Holies to atone for (cover) his sin and the national sins of the people of Israel. God prepared Joshua to fulfill the role of high priest once the temple was built.

5. According to Vision #4 in Zechariah 3:1-10, what did God do or say to encourage Joshua the high priest (who represented the people) to trust Him and follow His way?

- Verse 2—

- Verses 3-5—

- Verses 6-7—

- Verses 8-10—

> **Scriptural Insight:** The LORD explained that these garments symbolized the high priest's (Israel's) iniquities, which He had forgiven. He promised to remove His representative's filthy robes and replace them with festive robes, the apparel of royalty and wealth— symbolic of God's righteousness (cf. Isa. 3:22). Thus God would restore Israel so that she could fulfill her original calling as a priestly nation (cf. Exod. 19:6; Isa. 61:6). (*Dr. Constable's Notes on Zechariah 2022 Edition*, p. 42)

6. Read the following references related to the "Branch"—Isaiah 11:1 and Jeremiah 23:5. Who is "my servant, the Branch" (Zechariah 3:8)?

> **Focus on the Meaning:** The name *Jesus*, announced to Joseph and Mary through the angels (Matthew 1:21; Luke 1:31), comes from the Hebrew name *Yeshua* (meaning "Yahweh saves" or "Yahweh is salvation"). The English spelling of the Hebrew *Yeshua* is *Joshua*. When translated from Hebrew into Greek, the original language of the New Testament, the name *Yeshua* becomes *Iēsous*. In English, *Iēsous* becomes *Jesus*. Thus, *Yeshua* and, correspondingly, *Joshua* and *Jesus* mean "Yahweh saves" or "the Lord is salvation." (adapted from *"What is the meaning of the name Jesus?"* at gotquestions.org)

Read Zechariah 6:9-15.

7. What else do you learn about the Branch (verse 13)?

Scriptural Insight: In Jewish Law, tradition, and practice, the high priest and king were never combined into one role. That is why Psalm 110:4 foreshadows the dual role of the Messiah, "You are a priest forever, in the order of Melchizedek." Melchizedek in Genesis 14:18 was both a king and a priest of God.

8. Joshua was to be symbolically crowned in Jerusalem to represent the future Messiah as both king and priest. What do these verses say about Jesus fulfilling that role?

   • Luke 1:32-33—

   • Hebrews 6:19-20—

9. From both Zechariah 3:1-10 and 6:9-15, what did God do or say to encourage His people to trust Him and follow His way instead of the world's way or their own way?

Read Zechariah chapter 4.

10. According to Vision #5 in Zechariah 4:1-14, what did God do or say to encourage Zerubbabel to trust Him and follow His way instead of the world's way or their own way?

   • Verses 6-7—

   • Verses 8-10—

   Focus on the Meaning: This vision references God the Spirit. So together with Zechariah 3:1-10 and 6:9-15 (the Son), we see references to the Trinity here in the Old Testament.

Application for today

11. What God told Zerubbabel in Zechariah 4:6 still applies to us as believers today. Find New Testament verses that support this truth for Christians.

Your favorite verse(s) from today's study:

Respond to the Lord about what you learned today.

DAY THREE STUDY

Ask the Lord Jesus to teach you through His Word.

Additional Reading (Optional): Read Zechariah 5:1-6:8. What do you learn from each of these visions?

Vision #6 (Zechariah 5:1-4)—

Vision #7 (Zechariah 5:5-11)—

Vision #8 (Zechariah 6:1-8)—

---

2 years later; 518 B.C. while they are building the temple

Read Zechariah chapter 7.

12. From verses 1-2, what was challenging God's people, and what did they do about it?

13. What did God do or say to encourage them to trust Him and follow His way instead of the world's way or their own way?

- Verses 5-6—

- Verses 7-10—

- Verses 11-13—

> **Scriptural Insight:** The Jews were mourning the consequences of their forefathers' sin (the destruction of the temple and Jerusalem) rather than the sin itself. This also reflected how they had become content in the land without the presence of God represented by the temple—what Haggai addressed in Haggai chapter 1. Fasting was supposed to reveal their weakness and need for dependence on the Lord. The current Jews also needed to repent of their own sin and live in holiness representing God's holiness to all in the land.

Application for today

14. What do you learn about God in this lesson that encourages you today?

15. It is easy to wallow in past mistakes, getting caught in sinful behavior, and blaming others for what happened to you. Do you spend more time and emotion grieving the consequences of sinful choices rather than the sin that made that choice? Agree with God about the sin, accept His forgiveness through your faith in Christ, pursue obedience in that area of your life, and depend on the Lord to help you follow His way instead of the world's way or your own way. Rejoice as you move forward and live for Him.

Respond to the Lord about what you learned today.

DAY FOUR STUDY

Ask the Lord Jesus to teach you through His Word.

Read Zechariah chapter 8.

"This is what the Lord says" occurs ten times in this chapter. Most are promises of what He will do for His people.

16. According to Zechariah 8:1-6, what did God do or say to encourage His people to trust Him and follow His way instead of the world's way or their own way?

    • Verses 2-3—

    • Verses 4-6—

17. According to Zechariah 8:7-13, what did God do or say to encourage His people to trust Him and follow His way instead of the world's way or their own way?

    • Verse 7-9—

    • Verses 12-13—

18. According to Zechariah 8:14-19, what did God do or say to encourage His people to trust Him and follow His way instead of the world's way or their own way?

    • Verse 15—

    • Verses 16-17—

    • Verses 18-19—

19. According to Zechariah 8:20-23, what did God do or say to encourage all people to trust Him and follow His way instead of the world's way or their own way?

- Verses 20-22—

- Verse 23—

> **Scriptural Insight:** Jerusalem is no longer viewed simply as the heart of Judaism but as the center of God's dealings with all nations, and as a glorious realization of the ancient promise given to Abraham (cf. Gen. 12:3). (*Dr. Constable's Notes on Zechariah 2022 Edition*, p. 86)

Application for today

20. What do you learn about God in this lesson that encourages you today?

Your favorite verse(s) from today's study:

Respond to the Lord about what you learned today.

Recommended: Listen to the podcast "Zechariah—The Pervasive Power and Persistent Purpose of God" to reinforce what you have learned. Use the listener guide on the next page.

Zechariah—The Pervasive Power and Persistent Purpose of God

FINDING TREASURE IN ZECHARIAH

- What a joy to discover so much treasure in this relatively unknown book! The New Testament writers either quote or refer to verses in Zechariah more than forty-one times. One historian said that this was one of the favorite books of the early church Christians because it contains so many of God's promises about the coming Messiah.

- As a priest, Zechariah was already representing the people before God in his priestly duties. God called him to do more—to be a prophet. A prophet was God's mouthpiece to the people representing God through the words God gave him to share with the Jews then and everyone else who has lived since that time. That includes you and me today.

- God chose to deliver His messages through a lot of visions. Some of those visions are like the parables Jesus told—descriptions of recognizable aspects of life that had a truth to grasp and application to your faith walk. God uses colorful examples for us to illustrate what He wants us to know. Sometimes we remember the examples better than just straight teaching. Isn't that true?

  The whole book is a revelation of the pervasive power and the persistent purpose of Yahweh. ... People experiencing adversity frequently see only things that are close at hand. Zechariah provided hope from visions that he saw ... that encouraged his audience to lift their eyes to behold the larger plans and purposes of their God. (*Dr. Constable's Notes on Zechariah 2023 Edition,* p. 13)

- Through Zechariah, God revealed things about the future of the Jews that gave his discouraged contemporaries hope. God revealed things about Himself and our future that give us hope as well. We are to be confident in the pervasive power of God and the persistent purpose of God.

THE PERVASIVE POWER OF GOD

- Haggai, Zechariah, and Malachi refer to God as the "Lord Almighty." This title for God refers to Him being the sovereign Lord and Master of the entire universe. He was greater than any Persian emperor, the local governors, and other officials who opposed them.

- God's power was available first for His people as they trusted Him and followed His way more than their own way or the world's way. He wanted them to fully return to Him to receive future blessing from Him. That included not only what He would do for the current Jewish population but also His plans to come to His people in the person of their Messiah who would be His own Son. And God would provide the power for restoration of them as a people through His Spirit.

- God knew what His people 2500 years ago needed to bring them back to Him. Each one of the eight visions given to Zechariah revealed an aspect of God's pervasive power to overcome what Zechariah's audience faced and to give them hope.

- God does the same for you as His child. His pervasive power on your behalf overcomes whatever you are facing. Romans 8:31; Ephesians 3:16,20

  "This is the word of the Lord to Zerubbabel: 'Not by might nor by power, but by my Spirit,' says the Lord Almighty. (Zechariah 4:6)

- Through the power of His Spirit in us, we can succeed at anything God desires for us to do. The pervasive power of God will help us get through the challenges of life with hope.

THE PERSISTENT PURPOSE OF GOD

- God has a plan for human history. He works in the background of life to move history toward His intended goal. His purpose endures over any human or Satanic opposition. Nothing can thwart His purpose. Zechariah 2:8,10-11

- He would come to live among them not just in the temple but as a human—Emmanuel, which means God with us. Jesus Christ fulfilled that promise. And many nations have joined with the Lord through Christ and have become God's people, way beyond just the Jews. God's persistent purpose was fulfilled. *Zechariah 3:8-9*

- God removed sin in a single day through Jesus' death on the cross 550 years later. Believers in Jesus have our sin removed and replaced with Christ's rich clothes of righteousness. *Galatians 3:26-27*

- The future Messiah would be both a king and a priest for God's people. Jesus fulfilled God's persistent purpose in this prophecy. *Zechariah 6:11-13*

- God told them to be strong and finish building the temple because many people who desired God would head to Jerusalem to worship Him there at the temple. After Jesus' death and resurrection, people from all languages did come, heard the gospel message, experienced the day of Pentecost, and went back home to share the good news. God's persistent purpose was fulfilled. *Zechariah 8:20-2; Acts 2:1-6-11*

FOLLOWING GOD'S WAY

- When you have confidence in the pervasive power of God to handle any situation in your life, does that encourage you to follow His way of living life rather than the world's way?

- When you have confidence in the persistent purpose of God to do His work in His time, does that help you relax and trust Him to work His plan even if you cannot see the effects right now?

Let Jesus satisfy your heart with complete trust in Him so that you will follow His way of living life instead of the world's way or your own way.

Lesson 5: Ezra 5-6; Zechariah 9-14

518-516 B.C.

DAY ONE STUDY

Ask the Lord Jesus to teach you through His Word.

Historical Background

For the ABC's of Ezra, see Lesson 3.

The Babylonian exile began in 605 B.C. and ended in 536 B.C. when a group of 50,000 Jews headed home. The group that returned was chosen by God (Ezra 1:5). Once back in their homeland, the Jews rebuilt the altar in Jerusalem and started rebuilding the temple. They stopped the work when the Samaritans opposed the building and bribed the officials against the Jews. The work stopped for sixteen years.

During the sixteen intervening years, a lot of political upheaval took place in the Persian Empire—rulers being assassinated and overthrown one after another. Finally, in 522 B.C., Darius I (also known as Darius the Great) became king. He was one of Persian's most capable rulers, remembered for his administrative genius and great building projects. As an administrator, he completed Cyrus's organization of the empire into satraps (provinces); standardized coinage, weights, and measure; and developed land and sea routes for communication and commerce. All these steps helped to unite the diverse peoples while at the same time respecting their native religious institutions. He made Susa his administrative capital (as seen in Esther and Nehemiah) where he built an audience hall and a residential palace. His style of Persian architecture endured for almost 200 years. Darius attempted various times to conquer Greece without success, including his defeat at the famous battle of Marathon in 490 B.C. Under Darius's capable rule, the Jews in Jerusalem and Judah prospered.

Two years after Darius established his reign, God sent the prophets Haggai and Zechariah to encourage and support the high priest Joshua and the Jewish governor Zerubbabel to begin the building of the temple again. The message of God through Haggai was to stimulate in the people a desire for God's presence with them. Through Haggai, God also let them people know that He was pleased with Zerubbabel's efforts in returning the captives to Jerusalem and leading them to build the second temple. The message of Zechariah confirmed this as Zechariah anointed Joshua and Zerubbabel with power to do God's work or building the temple and leading the people. "Not by might, nor by power, but by my Spirit," says the Lord Almighty (Zechariah 4:6).

Read Ezra chapter 5.

1. What was challenging God's people (vv. 1-3)?

2. What choices did they make or need to make (vv. 5, 17)?

3. What did they boldly declare about their identity (v. 11)?

4. What did God do or say to encourage them to trust Him and follow His way instead of the world's way or their own way?

Read Ezra chapter 6.

We see in the beginning of chapter 6 the two aspects of trusting God. 1) The Jews believed God's Word through Haggai and Zechariah and kept building during the waiting. 2) They trusted God to work in the king's heart to find the decree and give his approval.

5. What did God do or say to encourage them to trust Him and follow His way instead of the world's way or their own way (vv. 1-13, 22)?

6. What did King Darius ask of the Jews (v. 10)?

7. How did the people respond?

    *   Verses 14-15—

- Verses 16-18—

- Verses 19-22—

Scriptural Insight: The temple was completed 60 years after its destruction. Older Jews who recalled the size and grandeur of the first temple wept as they compared Zerubbabel's temple (smaller and with less glitz) to the splendor of Solomon's temple. Also, Solomon's temple had housed the ark of the Covenant, which was apparently no longer in Israel's possession. At the first temple's dedication, the altar had been lit by fire from heaven, and the temple had been filled with the Shekinah glory. There is no record of such a miracle at the second temple's dedication. But Haggai records God promising to fill this new temple with His glory (Haggai 2:7) so we know that He did. And God promises that the second temple would one day have a magnificence to outshine the glory of the first (Haggai 2:8–9). God's promise was fulfilled 500 years later when the Messiah Himself (Jesus Christ) walked the courts of the temple that Zerubbabel built (and King Herod later refurbished). Jesus confirmed that God dwelled in the second temple (Matthew 23:21).

Application for today

8. Consider anything in this lesson that is similar to today. Find New Testament verses that you can apply in your life to that similar situation.

Your favorite verse(s) from today's study:

Respond to the Lord about what you learned today.

DAY TWO STUDY

Ask the Lord Jesus to teach you through His Word.

> For the ABC's of Zechariah and what was covered in chapters 1-8, see Lesson 4.

Note: We will not cover all of chapters 9-14 in detail. Feel free to read the rest on your own.

Read Zechariah 9:9-17.

9. What did God promise to His people to encourage them to trust Him and follow His way instead of the world's way or their own way (vv. 9-12)?

Scriptural Insight: Zechariah 9:9 was literally fulfilled by Jesus (Matthew 21:5; John 12:15). Zechariah 9:13 is likely a reference to the future victory of the Jews led by the Maccabee family over the wicked Greek kings in the second century B.C.

10. What did God promise to His people to encourage them to trust Him and follow His way instead of the world's way or their own way (vv. 14-17)?

Read Zechariah 10:1-12.

11. What do you learn about God in vv. 1-3?

12. What did God promise to His people to encourage them to trust Him and follow His way instead of the world's way or their own way?

- Verses 4-9—

- Verse 12—

Application for today

13. What, if anything, in this lesson encourages you today?

Your favorite verse(s) from today's study:

Respond to the Lord about what you learned today.

DAY THREE STUDY

Ask the Lord Jesus to teach you through His Word.

> *Additional Reading (Optional):* Read Zechariah 11. What do you learn?

Zechariah chapters 12-14 speak to the future of Jerusalem and Israel in the last days.
Read Zechariah chapter 12.

14. What do you learn about God in ...?

- Verses 1-3—

- Verses 5-6—

- Verse 9—

15. What will God do for future Jews (vv. 10-14)?

Read Zechariah chapter 13.

16. What do you learn about God in vv. 1-6?

17. What do you learn about God in vv. 7-9?

Application for today

18. What, if anything, in this lesson encourages you today?

Your favorite verse(s) from today's study:

Respond to the Lord about what you learned today.

DAY FOUR STUDY

Ask the Lord Jesus to teach you through His Word.

Read Zechariah chapter 14.

> **Focus on the Meaning:** The cosmic, eschatological sweep of this last portion ... is almost without compare in the prophetic literature of the OT for the richness of its imagery, the authority of its pronouncements, and the majestic exaltation of the God of Israel who will be worshiped as the God of all the earth. ... Zechariah announced that a day was coming for the LORD—coming primarily for His benefit—when the spoils that the nations had taken from the Israelites would be returned and divided among the Jews. This would be the LORD's day, in which He would do His will, in contrast to man's day, in which man conducts his affairs without divine interference. The day of the Lord in prophetic literature designates any time when Yahweh steps into the arena of human events to effect his purposes. (*Dr. Constable's Notes on Zechariah 2023 Edition,* p. 129)

19. What grabbed your attention from ...?

- Verses 3-5—

- Verses 6-8—

- Verses 9-11—

- Verse 16—

20. From chapters 12-14, what do you learn about God's involvement in human history including the future?

Focus on the Meaning: God grasps everything in a moment, the beginning, the middle, and the end of the entire human race and of all time. And what we consider and measure according to the sequence of time as a very long, extended tapeline, He sees in its entirety, as though wound together in a ball. (Martin Luther, *What Luther Says: An Anthology*)

Application for today

21. How should knowing the truths in Zechariah chapters 12-14 affect how you live and what you do and say today?

Your favorite verse(s) from today's study:

Respond to the Lord about what you learned today.

Recommended: Listen to the podcast "Zechariah—Your King Comes" to reinforce what you have learned. Use the listener guide on the next page.

Zechariah—Your King Comes

THE KING PRESENTS HIMSELF

Rejoice greatly, Daughter Zion! Shout, Daughter Jerusalem! See, your king comes to you, righteous and victorious, lowly and riding on a donkey, … His rule will extend from sea to sea and from the River to the ends of the earth. (Zechariah 9:9-10)

- The picture of the king riding on the donkey colt was significant. In the ancient Near East, rulers commonly rode donkeys if they came in peace. But they rode horses into war. Jesus was coming in peace to offer peace. But He was rejected as Israel's king.

- We have to wait until He returns before we see verse 10 fulfilled. God's persistent purpose is to have Jesus Christ as the Messiah to rule a kingdom on earth extending from Jerusalem to the ends of the earth. God will make that happen because He promised it.

SPARKLING IN GOD'S LAND

- Even though the Jews were under the control of other nations, God was working on their behalf. Regardless of who controlled the Promised Land, it belonged to God and still does. The Jewish people would need to trust God to deliver them from their enemies. When they did trust Him, they would recognize how God delivered them and then would sparkle in the LORD's land, like jewels in a crown. *Zechariah 9:16-17*

- Jesus is Lord of this planet. That means the place where you live belongs to Him. Believers should be attractive to the nonbelieving world. When we trust God and choose to follow His way rather than the world's way or our own way, we sparkle like jewels or stars in the sky. Others notice and are drawn to Him. *Philippians 2:14-16*

THE KING'S RETURN WITH POWER AND PURPOSE

- The Lord Almighty who is also Creator God and Life-Giver to every human has a plan that sounds crazy. All nations will lose their minds and fight against Jerusalem—a small city compared to the rest of the world's cities. Jerusalem represents God's presence on the earth and His authority over all humans. Only a persistent God could make such an insignificant piece of land a target for all the nations of the earth. *Zechariah 12:1-3*

- While that is happening, God will use His power to help His people return to Him. Many unbelieving Jews will recognize Jesus as their Messiah and trust in Him. *Zechariah 12:10; Romans 11:25-27*

- The Lord Almighty will fight for His people against those nations that target Jerusalem. *Zechariah 14:3-5*

- The Lord as Christ Jesus will come down from heaven himself and stand on the Mount of Olives. It will split in half from east to west likely along a fault already present there. The Lord will use the resulting valley as an escape route for His people and later as a river for spring-fed water. *Zechariah 14:8*

- We as believers in Christ will come with our Lord on this day. "Holy ones" refers to God's saints—everyone who believes in Christ and has received their resurrection bodies. We will be coming back with Him. *Zechariah 14:5; 1 Thessalonians 3:13; 4:14-17*

- The battle will be short and decisive. Jesus will defeat His enemies by His pervasive power. When it is over, He will be King of planet Earth. *Zechariah 14:9*

HOW CAN IT BE?

- Like Daniel, Zechariah gives a lot of detail about Israel's future—what God will make happen. There is no reason to believe the skeptics who denounce these Old Testament prophecies saying they were not written until after many of the events already happened.

  God grasps everything in a moment, the beginning, the middle, and the end of the entire human race and of all time. And what we consider and measure according to the sequence of time as a very long, extended tapeline, He sees in its entirety, as though wound together in a ball. (Martin Luther, What Luther Says: An Anthology)

- If you believe in the pervasive power of God and the persistent purpose of God, you can be confident that whatever God wants to happen will happen. God can always find a rebellious heart to do that which causes pain to others. God's Spirit can woo anyone with a tender heart toward Him to serve Him in human history. He has a plan that fulfills His purpose. He sees what He wants to accomplish in human history. He allows humans the freedom to make the choices for Him or against Him and work accordingly. That includes influencing parents to name their children to match what He has already promised about that person with that name.

WHAT IS YOUR RESPONSE?

- You and I need to receive the Lord as our King now. Instead of overly lamenting about any earthly political issue, we need to recognize who is truly King. That was important for the Jews to remember under the rule of the Persian emperors, and it is important for you to remember in your country today. You and I need to receive the Lord Jesus as King of our lives now!

> Note: To learn more about God's kingdom, listen to this podcast, "Jesus and the Kingdom of God."

Let Jesus satisfy your heart with complete trust in Him so that you will follow His way of living life instead of the world's way or your own way.

Lesson 6: Esther 1-10

483-473 B.C.

DAY ONE STUDY

ABCs of Esther

Author

The title of this book comes from its principal character, Esther. The author is unstated and unknown. The historian Josephus gave the writing credit to Mordecai, a principal character in the book and relative of the main character Esther. References in the book show that he were familiar with Persian culture and literature (Esther 2:23; 10:2). The writer was likely a Jew and wrote as though he was an eyewitness of the events he recorded. Mordecai did record certain matters and sent letters to other Jews concerning them (Esther 9:20). Other sources for the book include the books of the Chronicles of the Median and Persian kings (Esther 2:23; 6:1; 10:2). Another possible candidate for author is Nehemiah who served the next king in Susa thirty years later.

> **Historical Insight:** The writer could have written it any time after 473 B.C., the year the Jews defended themselves and instituted the Feast of Purim, the last historical events in the book (9:27-28). If a contemporary of these events composed it, he probably did so within a generation or two of this date. The first extra-biblical reference to the book is in 2 Maccabees 15:36, which dates from late in the second century B.C., so we know it was written before then. (*Dr. Constable's Notes on Esther 2022 Edition,* pp. 1-2)

Background

In 539 B.C. Babylon fell to the Persian monarch Cyrus the Great. Nearly two centuries before, Isaiah had predicted the rise of Cyrus (Isaiah 45:1). When Cyrus conquered Babylon, he decreed that God's people could return to Judea and rebuild their temple in Jerusalem. Three groups of people returned—the first led by Zerubbabel in 537 B.C., the second led by Ezra 80 years later (457 B.C.), and the third group came with Nehemiah 15 years after that. The new temple was completed in 516 B.C.

Most of the Jews in exile did not return, even though they had been encouraged to do so by God's prophets before the exile began (Isaiah 48:20; Jeremiah 50:8; 51:6). They were to return to the place where the Lord could bless them under the covenantal promises (Deuteronomy 28). But many of the exiled Jews continued in the life as they had come to know it outside the Promised Land. Esther and Mordecai were among those who chose not to return. In 1893, an archaeological expedition discovered some ancient documents revealing how wealthy and influential some of the Jews who remained in Babylon were.

The book of Esther concerned those who remained in Babylon and other parts of the Persian Empire apart from Israel between the time of Zerubbabel and Ezra. The events took place during the reign of the Persian King Ahasuerus (486-465 B.C.) also known as Xerxes who was a strong, effective ruler. The first historical event to which the writer alluded seems to be Ahasuerus' military planning session, at which he plotted the strategy for his ill-fated campaign against Greece (Esther 1:3-21). The king held this planning session in the winter of 483-482 B.C. The last recorded event in Esther is the institution of the Feast of Purim, which took place in 473 B.C. Therefore, the events recorded in the book span a period of about nine or 10 years and fit chronologically between Ezra chapters 6 and 7.

Context

In the English Bible, Esther follows Ezra and Nehemiah with the historical books. But in the Hebrew Bible, it is one of five short books that appear toward the end of the biblical writings. The problem with Esther was the absence of any direct mention of God. Some questioned whether a book that did not mention God could be considered sacred scripture.

> **Scriptural Insight:** Although the book does not directly mention God, it would be difficult to read it without sensing the providence of God working in powerful, though at times subtle, ways to rescue his people from danger and possible extermination. (*The New English Translation Bible*, 2019 ed., note on 1:1)

The New Testament does not quote from the book of Esther. The Law is never mentioned in the book. Neither are sacrifices, offerings, or prayers to God mentioned, unlike the other postexilic books (Ezra and Nehemiah). Some suggest that the Jews who did not return lacked spiritual awareness except in their assurance that God would protect His people. The book of Esther did remind the Jews of the faithfulness of God to His people and explained how the Feast of Purim began.

The map below identifies some of the Persian cities mentioned in the book of Esther. The Empire was about as wide as the continental United States.

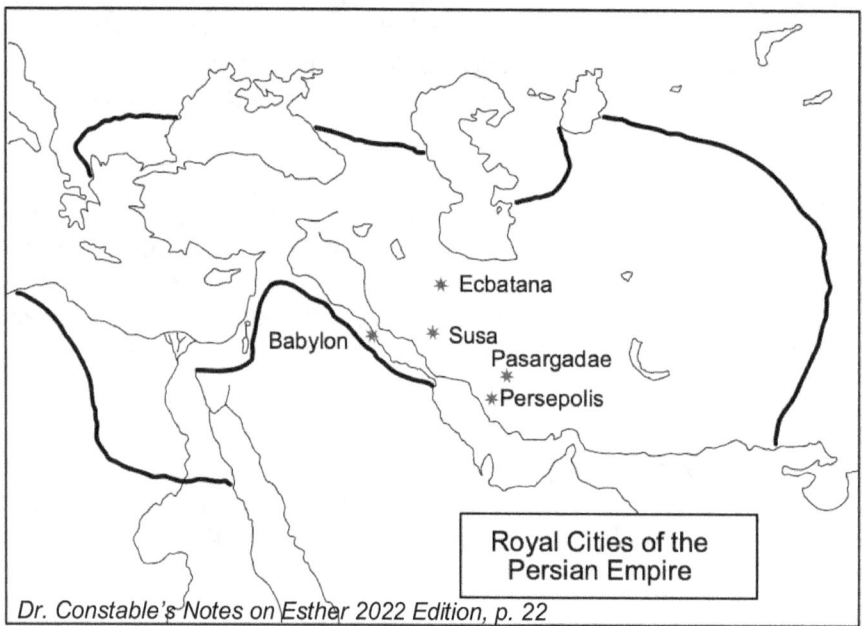

Dr. Constable's Notes on Esther 2022 Edition, p. 22

Ask the Lord Jesus to teach you through His Word.

483 B.C.

Read Esther chapter 1.

> **Historical Insight:** Ahasuerus is the Hebrew name of the Persian king Xerxes. He reigned over the Persian Empire from 486 to 465 B.C. and was the son of Darius I (521-486 B.C.). Xerxes is famous in secular history for two things: his defeat at the hands of the Greeks (480-479 B.C.), and his building of the royal palace at Persepolis. Xerxes was also known for his drinking, lavish banquets, and harsh temper.

1. What do you learn about King Xerxes and the Persian Empire from chapter 1?

483-479 B.C.

Read Esther chapter 2.

> **Historical Insight:** Mordecai's great grandfather Kish had been carried into Babylonian exile in 597 B.C. Mordecai was born after that time.

2. What was challenging Esther and Mordecai in vv. 1-18?

> **Historical Insight:** The queenship was an honorary/political position. The king was a polygamist with many wives and concubines in his harem, but the queen was a special wife occupying a favored position. Like Daniel and his friends, Esther was likely a young teenager when forcibly taken into the king's harem. The harem system was, and still is, a horrible system. In essence, after [the virgins] had been violated, they became slaves and virtual widows. A woman whom Xerxes never called again would live her life in the harem as a pampered prisoner with no possibility for a real marriage or family of her own unless she became pregnant. (adapted from various sources)

3. What choices did they make or need to make?

- Esther—

- Mordecai—

4. What happened in vv. 19-23? How did Mordecai respond?

Application for today

5. Consider anything in this lesson that is similar to today. Find New Testament verses that you can apply in your life to that similar situation.

Your favorite verse(s) from today's study:

Respond to the Lord about what you learned today.

DAY TWO STUDY

Ask the Lord Jesus to teach you through His Word.

Four years later

Read Esther chapter 3.

6. What choice did Mordecai make (vv. 1-4)?

7. What happened as a result (vv. 6-15)?

Historical Insight: This is a complete departure from all the actions of the Babylonian and Persian leaders before. The rulers up to this point had allowed the religious differences from all the different people groups under their rule. Because of Haman's hatred and because Xerxes needs the money, the Jewish people are facing the worst ethnic cleansing in their history to this point—at least all those known to be practicing Jews. (Wayne Braudrick, "A Woman of Courage," sermon on November 15, 2015)

We already saw in Daniel 3:8-12 and Daniel 6:4-9 other instances of evil advisors appealing to a king's pride in order to exact some reaction from the king that would destroy mainly Jews. Haman is another such evil advisor appealing to a king's pride and need for money!

Read Esther chapter 4.

8. What choices did Mordecai and Esther make or need to make?

- Mordecai (vv. 6-8)—

- Esther (vv. 9-11)—

- Mordecai (vv. 12-14)—

- Esther (vv. 15-16)—

Focus on the Meaning: Fasting does not please God to force Him to move His hand to do what we ask (as in paganism). We fast so we will be starving hungry to remind ourselves how incredibly weak we are and then partner that fast with prayer enjoining the presence of God who is ultimately in charge. (Wayne Braudrick, "A Woman of Courage," sermon on November 15, 2015)

Read Esther chapter 5.

9. How did Esther do her part God's way while trusting God to do His part in the king's heart (verses 1-8)?

Application for today

10. When have you found yourself in a similar situation where you were given a "God moment" to make a difference in the lives of others? Describe how you recognized the opportunity and what happened. Did you respond in a God-honoring way while trusting God to do His part?

Think About It: The real test of courage is trusting God in a world like ours where evil seems to surround the righteous and even justice comes out perverted. (Wayne Braudrick, "A Woman of Courage," sermon on November 15, 2015)

11. Consider anything in this lesson that is similar to today. Find New Testament verses that you can apply in your life to that similar situation.

Your favorite verse(s) from today's study:

Respond to the Lord about what you learned today.

DAY THREE STUDY

Ask the Lord Jesus to teach you through His Word.

Read Esther chapter 6.

12. What did God make happen in His perfect timing that benefited Mordecai (vv. 1-3, 10-11)?

13. What insight did Haman's wife Zeresh have about the Jews that Haman ignored (v. 13)?

Read Esther chapter 7.

14. How did Esther respond to the opportunity God gave to her (vv. 1-6)?

15. How did the king respond to Esther's revelation?

Read Esther chapter 8.

16. What did God do to help His people even though He is not mentioned (vv. 1-8)?

17. What was the result (vv. 16-17)? How did that glorify God?

Application for today

18. Consider anything in this lesson that is similar to today. Find New Testament verses that you can apply in your life to that similar situation.

Your favorite verse(s) from today's study:

Respond to the Lord about what you learned today.

DAY FOUR STUDY

Ask the Lord Jesus to teach you through His Word.

Read Esther chapter 9.

19. What choices did God's people make?

20. What did God do to help them even though He is not mentioned?

21. How did God use Queen Esther to work on behalf of His people (vv. 29-32)?

Think About It: The plot once intended to destroy the Jews resulted in the Feast of Purim which helped to unite and sustain them as a people. And God used this opportunity to bring nonbelievers to faith in Himself. A win-win for all!

Read Esther chapter 10.

22. What did the king do that benefited the Jews?

Think About It: Mordecai acted as Joseph and Daniel did in becoming second in command under a pagan king. All three used their influence to benefit God's people.

Application for today

23. Read 1 Peter 5: 6-7. How do the lives of Esther and Mordecai in their responses to challenges and subsequent rewards illustrate this passage?

24. Consider anything else in this lesson that is similar to today. Find New Testament verses that you can apply in your life to that similar situation.

Your favorite verse(s) from today's study:

Respond to the Lord about what you learned today.

Recommended: Listen to the podcast "Esther—Trusting God to Work in the Background" to reinforce what you have learned. Use the listener guide on the next page.

Esther—Trusting God to Work in the Background

THE LIFE-OR-DEATH CHALLENGE

- Esther was forcibly taken out of her home and put into the king's harem, a horrible system. She could trust God, obey the king's order, and be the best women she could be in her situation. Or she could consider herself a victim and be miserable. Esther chose to do her part God's way by being the best woman she could be, honoring Mordecai. *Esther 2:20*

- God did His part by having the king choose her to be his queen. God worked on the king so that he trusted Esther. Her presence in the palace also helped to save the king's life. And God had a plan to use Esther again for His purposes later. *Esther 2:22*

- Four years later, Mordecai notified Esther that all the Jews would be killed in 11 months. Mordecai challenged her to act on behalf of her people using her position. *Esther 2:8; 3:13; 4:12-14*

ESTHER RESPONDED GOD'S WAY

- Esther responded by doing her part God's way. She called for all Jews including herself to fast for three days, asking them to join her in prayer about what she could and should do. She was ready to obey God as her authority as she had obeyed Mordecai all her life. *Esther 4:15-16*

- Esther needed God's guidance as she did her part, which was to approach the king of Persia about this threat to her people. She needed God to do His part in directing the heart and mind of the king to receive her. She trusted the results in His hand.

- When God places something in your heart to do, especially when it involves someone else and situations over which you have no control, you must trust God to lead you in what you choose to do. You want to do your part His way, not your own way or the world's way.

- It is very easy to take an acceptable cultural practice and adapt it to whatever you are facing. You can know how to act according to God's way through His Word. He shows you how to do what is right.

ESTHER ACTED GOD'S WAY

- Trusting God, Esther did her part by approaching the king the right way, making sure he could see her, and waiting for his response. She did not force herself into the king's presence, demanding his attention. *Esther 5:1-2*

- God took care of His part by directing the king's heart and mind to be favorable to Esther's presence and her request. King Xerxes invited her into the chamber and asked what she wanted from him.

- Esther's part was to invite the king and Haman to a banquet. God worked through the king to grant Esther's request and accept her invitation. Those are the two aspects of trusting God.

OPPOSITION TESTED ESTHER'S TRUST

- Completely trusting God and doing things God's way do not stop the opposition. Esther's invitation included Haman—the enemy, the one who initiated the attack on the Jews. Yet, she did her part God's way while trusting that God would do His part in making the king respond favorably to her request to save her people.

- Learning to live dependently on your God does not guarantee that He will stop the opposition against you. He places that desire in your heart. He wants you to be obedient in carrying it out. But He does not necessarily make it easy. Why is that? After all, you could get the task or the service done more quickly without the delays and derision. Why doesn't God stop the opposition? Paul learned the answer to this.

  *But this happened that we might **not rely on ourselves but on God,** who raises the dead. (2 Corinthians 1:9)*

- Suffering, hardship, or opposition happens so we will learn to rely on God more than on ourselves. That does not mean we are to sit back and do nothing while waiting for God to do everything. Although, sometimes we need to pray and wait for the right moment to act as Esther did. That is trusting Him while we are waiting, praying, and seeking guidance.

GOD AVENGED THE WRONG DONE TO MORDECAI

- Haman hated Mordecai and was planning to have him executed. But God would take care of that too. The king could not sleep, so he asked for the journal of his reign to be read. God worked it out so that the reading included Mordecai's heroism to save the king. That is a work of God in the background, not a coincidence. *Esther 6:1-2*

- The king chose to honor Mordecai publicly and made the enemy Haman do it. That is God at work in the background also. *Esther 6:10*

- After Haman's death, he king continued to trust Esther and Mordecai, allowing them to draft whatever was needed to overcome the edict to kill the Jews. The Jews were saved, and the people were united in a celebration of joy.

THE TWO ASPECTS OF TRUSTING GOD

- God did not make it easy for Esther to stand up for her people. Likewise, you may find yourself in situations that seem beyond your ability to handle or control. God may not choose to rescue you from that opposition.

- But you can take action by responding God's way. And you can trust Him to do His part alongside what you are doing. Celebrate the victories!

Let Jesus satisfy your heart with complete trust in Him so that you will follow His way of living life instead of the world's way or your own way

Lesson 7: Ezra 7-10

458 B.C.

DAY ONE STUDY

Ask the Lord Jesus to teach you through His Word.

> For the ABC's of Ezra, see Lesson 3.

458 B.C. 60 years after the temple dedication (Ezra 4); 15 years after the failed attempt to wipe out the Jews (Esther 8-9).

Read Ezra chapter 7.

> **Historical Insight:** Artaxerxes (the son of King Xerxes who married Esther) was king of Persia from 464 to 425 B.C. His rule was peaceful, and his tolerant policy toward the Jews contributed to his role in repairs made to the temple and the walls of Jerusalem. In the seventh year of his reign, he sent Ezra to Jerusalem to support the Jewish people in their religious practices and worship at the temple. A few years later, enemies of the Jews sent Artaxerxes a letter denouncing the Jews as loyal citizens which led to a halt to the repairs being made to the walls of Jerusalem. Shortly after that, Artaxerxes gave permission for Nehemiah to go to Jerusalem and repair the walls.

1. What do you learn about Ezra in vv. 1-11?

   - Verses 1-6, 11—

   - Verses 7-11—

> **Focus on the Meaning:** Before the exile, scribes served the kings as secretaries or prophets by writing down what the prophet spoke. Post-exile, scribes became scholars who studies and taught the Scriptures. In the gospels, the terms scribes, lawyers, and teachers of the law all refer to this group of scholars. (adapted from *NIV Study Bible* note on Ezra 7:6)

2. What did God do through the king's decree to encourage His people to trust Him and follow His way instead of the world's way or their own way (vv. 11-26)?

   - Verses 12-13—

- Verses 14-20—

- Verses 21-26—

3. How did Ezra and the people respond (vv. 27-28)?

Dependent Living: Ezra was a very learned man with amazing humility. His humility led him to obedience to God and dependence on God. Six times in chapters 7 and 8, Ezra recognizes the "gracious hand of God was on him" (Ezra 7:6, 9, 28; 8:18, 22, 31). That is dependent living.

Application for today

4. Consider anything in this lesson that is similar to today. Find New Testament verses that you can apply in your life to that similar situation.

Your favorite verse(s) from today's study:

Respond to the Lord about what you learned today.

Day Two Study

Ask the Lord Jesus to teach you through His Word.

Read Ezra 8:15-36.

5. What was challenging God's people?

- Verse 15—

- Verses 21-13—

- Verses 24-30—

Scriptural Insight: Priests, like Ezra, had to descend from Moses' brother Aaron. Levites were from the tribe of Levi but not descended from Aaron. Levites served on a rotating basis to assist the priests with these duties: maintaining the temple grounds, opening or closing the doors in the morning/evening, keeping charge of the chambers and supply rooms on either side of the temple, guarding the temple treasury, and baking the 12 loaves of bread displayed inside the temple representing the 12 tribes of Israel. Temple servants were a group of people tasked with assisting the Levites in service of the temple. They did the menial work such as cutting wood and carrying water. David designated this group from non-Jews who were assimilated into the Jewish culture and vowed to follow the Jewish God.

6. What choices did they make or need to make?

- Verses 15-20—

- Verses 21-23—

- Verses 24-30—

7. What did God do or say to encourage them to trust Him and follow His way instead of the world's way or their own way?

8. How did the people respond (vv. 32-36)?

Application for today

9. Consider anything in this lesson that is similar to today. Find New Testament verses that you can apply in your life to that similar situation.

Your favorite verse(s) from today's study:

Respond to the Lord about what you learned today.

DAY THREE STUDY

Ask the Lord Jesus to teach you through His Word.

Read Ezra chapter 9.

10. What was challenging God's people (vv. 1-2)?

Scriptural Insight: Through Moses in Exodus 34:15-16, God warned His people about making treaties with the non-Jews in the land and arranging marriages with them. This did not apply to anyone who joined the Jews as proselytes and chose to worship God alone (i.e., Rahab and Ruth who married Jewish men)

11. What choices did they make or need to make (vv. 1, 3-5)?

12. In his prayer, what did Ezra acknowledge about…?

- The Jews (vv. 6-7)—

- God (vv. 8-9, 13, 15)—

Focus on the Meaning: Ezra knows that the people needed God's mercy. Mercy is not getting what you deserve for your sin (punishment). God offers every believer mercy today because of your faith in His Son. You are saved from the punishment that God requires for sin. Praise Him for His mercy!

Application for today

13. Consider anything in this lesson that is similar to today. Find New Testament verses that you can apply in your life to that similar situation.

Your favorite verse(s) from today's study:

Respond to the Lord about what you learned today.

DAY FOUR STUDY

Ask the Lord Jesus to teach you through His Word.

Read Ezra 10:1-19, 44.

14. How did the people respond to Ezra's prayer (vv. 1-2)?

15. What choices did they make or need to make (vv. 3-8)?

Historical Insight: This proposal is harsh in the light of modern Christian conceptions. Why should innocent children be punished? We must remember that the religious influence of the mothers on their children was regarded as the stumbling block. To keep the religion of the Lord pure was the one and only aim of Ezra and the returned exiles. As a small minority group, the repatriates lived in the Holy Land among a large population of influential people who were followers of various polytheistic religions. Against such larger numbers they had to defend themselves and their religious identity. Thus the drastic measures are understandable. (*Dr. Constable's Notes on Ezra 2023 Edition,* p. 65)

16. How did the people respond?

- Verses 9-14—

- Verse 15—

- Verses 16-19—

Scriptural Insight: The committee completed its work in three months, discovering that about 110 men were guilty of marrying pagan wives. (*NIV Study Bible,* note on Ezra 10:16-17, p. 690)

Application for today

17. Consider anything in this lesson that is similar to today. Find New Testament verses that you can apply in your life to that similar situation.

Your favorite verse(s) from today's study:

Respond to the Lord about what you learned today.

Recommended: Listen to the podcast "Ezra-Follow God's Way Rather Than Your Own Way" to reinforce what you have learned. Use the listener guide on the next page.

Ezra-Follow God's Way Rather Than Your Own Way

FOLLOWING GOD'S WAY OF PREPARATION

- Ezra devoted himself to the study and observance of the Law of Moses and prepared himself to teach it to the people about God in Israel. Ezra gathered other Jews to go with him, especially those involved in temple worship. *Ezra 7:6-7, 10*

- The king recognized that Ezra could benefit the people who were part of his kingdom then wrote a letter of recommendation for him. The king gave Ezra authority to use resources from his royal treasuries and to take freewill offerings from the people to do whatever was needed for the worship of God. The king declared that the priests, Levites, and temple workers were exempt from paying taxes. *Ezra 7:13-17*

- The king trusted Ezra and gave him authority to appoint judges to administer justice and to teach the people to obey God's Law and the king's law. *Ezra 7:25-26*

- Ezra praised the Lord for such a great privilege, and gathered leaders from Israel to go with him. Ezra chose to follow God's way and experienced the rewards. *Ezra 7:27-28*

FOLLOWING GOD'S WAY ON THE JOURNEY

- Ezra did his part by seeking volunteers God's way. God did His part by sending a group of Levites willing to go back to Israel. The group prayed for God to provide protection then traveled with confidence in God who did give them protection. Once in Jerusalem, they rested for three days. You can trust Him to take care of things while you rest. *Ezra 8:31-32*

- Ezra trusted God to help him find trustworthy people in their group who would guard all the riches they were carrying. Once in Jerusalem, they weighed out everything and put it in the hands of the priest and his associates. They managed the riches according to God's way and were found faithful. *Ezra 8:34*

- Ezra delivered the king's letter to the local officials as he was told to do by the king. That is God's way of dealing with the proper authorities. Ezra trusted God to do His part in making the officials agreeable to Ezra's presence and work there. *Ezra 8:36*

- Do you trust God with those things as well?

  - ✓ Recruiting volunteers—Do you seek out trustworthy people who can direct you to the right volunteers while trusting God to put a desire in their hearts to serve?

  - ✓ Travel—Do you seek God's protection as well as taking proper precautions? Or do you just trust in your own skills to handle anything.

  - ✓ Financial integrity—Do you ask God to lead you to trustworthy people to handle your finances and resources whether personal or business?

  - ✓ Respecting authority—Do you approach authorities with respect and honesty while trusting God to work on their hearts to accept whatever you are asking of them?

FOLLOWING GOD'S WAY IN CONFRONTING SIN

- A few months later, Ezra got hit with news of a terrible sin that a number of people were openly committing, even the priests who should have known better. Some of them had intermarried with the pagans in the land. Ezra mourned the sin, then confessed the sin, taking the guilt upon himself even though he was not guilty. He sought God's mercy for them. He met this challenge of sin by calling it what it was—sin! He did not accept their excuses. *Ezra 10:2-4*

- God worked on the hearts of the people to present a solution—separating from the pagan wives. Ezra selected trustworthy men to oversee the separations needed then trusted God to oversee their work and the people's responses. Within three months, it was done. All but two men agreed to give up their foreign wives.

- Confronting sin takes courage and conviction. Our culture tends to dismiss the seriousness of human sinfulness. We blame people and circumstances for our behavior and attitudes rather than taking responsibility for our own sinful choices. God hates sin. But God loves people. Jesus Christ came to take on our sin and incur the anger of God for us. Anyone who trusts in Christ receives this pardon for sin. The amazing thing is that God declares every believer "not guilty" even while we are capable of sinning again. Love of God and gratitude for what He has done should motivate us to obey Him and avoid sin in our lives.

- If you are in a leadership position, you must trust God by doing your part God's way. That would be to start with personal interaction as sisters in Christ. Then, bring others along who will lovingly confront the issue with you. You trust God to work on that person's heart to respond, to acknowledge the sin, and to turn from it through repentance and dependence on Christ to obey Him in that area of life. The goal is restoration of obedience to the Lord first which should lead to the restoration of community. *Matthew 18:15-17*

THE BLESSED REWARD

- By following God's way of preparing himself and leading others, Ezra was rewarded with seeing that the majority of the people turned from their sinful behavior. They then recommitted themselves to following God's way to live rather than the world's way or their own way. For a godly leader, that is a blessed reward.

Let Jesus satisfy your heart with complete trust in Him so that you will follow His way of living life instead of the world's way or your own way.

Lesson 8: Nehemiah 1-6

445-444 B.C.

DAY ONE STUDY

ABC's of Nehemiah

Author

The book of Nehemiah is a personal account written by Nehemiah himself. No information is given about Nehemiah's childhood, his adolescent years, or his family except for his father's name (Hacaliah) and one brother (Hanani). It is possible that his great grandparents had been taken captive to Babylon when Jerusalem fell 150 years earlier.

Nehemiah may have been born in Persia during or soon after Zerubbabel's governorship of Jerusalem. Like Daniel, he rose to a position of prominence in his pagan environment. He served King Artaxerxes as his personal cupbearer (Nehemiah 1:11). Soon he took on the role of wall-builder in Jerusalem and then governor of the Persian province of Judah (Nehemiah 1:1—2:20; 13:4-31).

> **Historical Insight:** This important position in the king's court gives us insight into Nehemiah's life and character. A mighty monarch such as the king of Persia would select for that position a man who was wise and discreet, and consistently honest and trustworthy. Nehemiah's position alone reveals much about his intellectual capabilities, his emotional maturity, and his spiritual status. (*The Bible Knowledge Commentary Old Testament,* p. 674)

Background

It had been almost 100 years since the first group of Jews returned to Judah in 538 B.C. under the leadership of Zerubbabel (Ezra 1:1-2:2). As you learned in Lesson 7, the returnees completed the rebuilding of the temple in 515 B.C. Ezra, the priest, then led another group back to Jerusalem sixty years later. Through Ezra's faithful teaching ministry, the majority of the people turned from their sinful behavior and recommitted themselves to following God's will for their lives. They must have also started to rebuild the city walls but were stopped by the opposition once again (Ezra 4:7-23).

In 445 B.C. (the twentieth year of Artaxerxes' reign, Nehemiah 1:1), Nehemiah learned of the conditions in Jerusalem that led him to request permission to return to Judah (Nehemiah 2:5). He arrived in Jerusalem in 444 B.C., fourteen years after Ezra's arrival bringing more Jewish exiles with him. God used Nehemiah to guide Judah in rebuilding the city's walls, completed in just 52 days (Nehemiah 6:15), and in reordering the people's social and economic lives. What he accomplished in a brief period of time was an incredible feat. Nehemiah stayed dependent on God and stayed focused on his task to accomplish this goal.

After twelve years in Jerusalem, Nehemiah returned home to Artaxerxes (432 B.C.) then came back to Jerusalem a year or two later. The record of his reforms following that return is in the last chapter of the book. Nehemiah probably wrote his book about 430 B.C. or shortly thereafter.

Context

Nehemiah follows Ezra among the historical books in the Old Testament. The two books are closely connected. A single story begins in Ezra and ends in Nehemiah.

This book covers the years 445-431 B.C. Even though the book spans about 15 years, most of the activity that Nehemiah recorded took place in 445-444 B.C. (chapters 1—12) and in 432- 431 B.C. (chapter 13). Together, Ezra and Nehemiah record about 110 years of Israel's history (538-430 B.C.). Nehemiah carries us to the end of the Old Testament chronologically. The historicity of this book has been well established by discoveries of ancient documents containing names included in the book.

Ask the Lord Jesus to teach you through His Word.

446 B.C. 12 years after Ezra arrived in Jerusalem

Read Ezra 4:6-23.

> **Historical Insight:** Though inserted in the book of Ezra before rebuilding of the temple began (520 B.C.), this letter fits in the time period when Artaxerxes was king. The Jews mentioned in this letter (v. 12) would have been those who returned with Ezra in 458 B.C., the second group of Jews to leave Babylon. That group attempted to rebuild the walls of the city, having received permission from Artaxerxes in 458 B.C. to do so (7:21). (*Dr. Constable's Notes on Ezra 2023 Edition* p. 39)

Read Nehemiah chapter 1.

1. What was challenging God's people—especially Nehemiah (v. 3)?

> **Focus on the Meaning:** The lack of walls around the city of Jerusalem left the city defenseless and stopped the progress of renewal of the city so that few people had chosen to live there. It was also embarrassing because Jerusalem represented their God.

2. What choices did Nehemiah make or need to make?

3. What did Nehemiah declare about God and ask of God (verses 5-11)?

Read Nehemiah chapter 2.

4. What was challenging Nehemiah (vv. 1-3)?

5. What choice did Nehemiah make (vv. 4-5)?

6. What did God do or say to encourage Nehemiah to trust Him and follow His way instead of the world's way or his own way (vv. 6-9)?

7. What challenge did Nehemiah face when he arrived in Jerusalem (vv. 10-20)?

> **Historical Insight:** Persian territory was divided into smaller provinces for management each with a "governor" appointed by the king. Sanballat was the governor of Samaria and the chief political opponent of Nehemiah. Tobiah was governor of Transjordan. His name and those of his children imply he worshiped Yahweh, though perhaps along with his native gods. He had a close relationship with Eliashib the priest, and his daughter married into one of the leading Jewish families. In his actions, however, Tobiah did everything he could to stop Nehemiah from fulfilling God's purpose for the Jews. (*NIV Study Bible,* note on Nehemiah 2:10, pp. 695-696)

8. What choices did Nehemiah make as he trusted God to lead him (vv. 11-20)?

9. How did the people respond (v. 18)?

Application for today

10. Consider anything in this lesson that is similar to today. Find New Testament verses that you can apply in your life to that similar situation.

Your favorite verse(s) from today's study:

Respond to the Lord about what you learned today.

DAY TWO STUDY

Ask the Lord Jesus to teach you through His Word.

Skim Nehemiah chapter 3.

11. What grabbed your attention?

Read Nehemiah chapter 4.

12. What was challenging God's people?

- Verses 1-6—

- Verses 7-15—

13. What choices did they make or need to make?

- Verses 1-6—

- Verses 7-15—

- Verses 16-23—

Focus on the Meaning: Fear is a normal human emotion designed by God to alert you to danger so that you will take action against it. As seen throughout this study, taking precautions against whatever is threatening you is part of trusting God by doing your part His way. Then, you trust God to do His part of protecting you. That is what Nehemiah and the Jews did in this chapter in response to the danger.

14. What did God do or say to encourage them to trust Him and follow His way instead of the world's way or their own way?

15. How did the people respond?

Application for today

16. Consider anything in this lesson that is similar to today. Find New Testament verses that you can apply in your life to that similar situation.

Your favorite verse(s) from today's study:

Respond to the Lord about what you learned today.

DAY THREE STUDY

Ask the Lord Jesus to teach you through His Word.

Read Nehemiah 5.

17. What was challenging God's people?

18. What choices did they make or need to make?

   • Nehemiah—

● The guilty ones—

19. What did God do or say to encourage them to trust Him and follow His way instead of the world's way or their own way?

20. How did they respond?

● The guilty ones—

● Nehemiah—

Scriptural Insight: In Mark 10:42-44, Jesus contrasted the dictatorial leadership styles of those who do not know God with the servant-leadership style that God wants for those who serve Him. Nehemiah was a servant-leader. Also, Romans 12:17-21 teaches that we should not take revenge but give that to God for Him to act according to His own way and timing. Nehemiah did that too.

Application for today

21. Consider anything in this lesson that is similar to today. Find New Testament verses that you can apply in your life to that similar situation.

Your favorite verse(s) from today's study:

Respond to the Lord about what you learned today.

DAY FOUR STUDY

Ask the Lord Jesus to teach you through His Word.

Read Nehemiah 6:1-19.

22. What was challenging God's people?

- Verses 1-4—

- Verses 5-9—

- Verses 10-14—

- Verses 16-19—

23. What choices did Nehemiah make or need to make?

- Verses 1-4—

- Verses 5-9—

- Verses 10-14—

- Verses 16-19—

24. What did God do or say to encourage Nehemiah to trust Him and follow His way instead of the world's way or his own way?

25. How did Nehemiah respond?

Application for today

26. Consider anything in this lesson that is similar to today. Find New Testament verses that you can apply in your life to that similar situation.

Your favorite verse(s) from today's study:

Respond to the Lord about what you learned today.

Recommended: Listen to the podcast "Nehemiah-Trusting God with Lies, Dangers, and a Really Hard Job" to reinforce what you have learned. Use the listener guide on the next page.

Nehemiah-Trusting God with Lies, Dangers, and a Really Hard Job

LIES STOPPED PROGRESS IN JERUSALEM

- Fake news is sprinkled throughout the books of Ezra and Nehemiah. It always has the purpose of discouraging God's people from doing the work He gave them to do.

- The non-Jews who had political power over the provinces of Judah and its neighbors in the Persian Empire told lies to the king about the Jews attempting to rebuild their city. He believed the fake news that his tax income would disappear. The king put a halt to the building. *Ezra 4:13,16,23-24*

NEHEMIAH RESPONDED TO GOD'S CALL

- Nehemiah heard that the city of Jerusalem was in shambles. Nehemiah mourned the condition of Jerusalem and prayed about what to do for four months.

- After that time of prayer, God placed into Nehemiah's heart the desire to go and repair the walls and gates of Jerusalem. Nehemiah prayed for a specific response from God as he approached the king. *Nehemiah 1:11*

- Nehemiah boldly approached the king, letting the king know of his sadness. He appealed to the king's favor and asked for the king to actually send him to the city of Jerusalem. Then, Nehemiah asked for letters to all the authorities for safe travel, for materials needed to rebuild the walls, and for a residence for himself in Jerusalem. Nehemiah recognized how God worked alongside what he was doing. *Nehemiah 2:5,8*

- As a trusted friend and advisor to the king, Nehemiah was sent by the king as Governor of Judah with an army to back him up. He arrived in Jerusalem and told the people what he had come to do. The people responded favorably to this outsider sent by the king who would be their leader in a really hard job they would do. *Nehemiah 2:17-18*

OPPOSITION TESTED NEHEMIAH'S TRUST

- Completely trusting God and doing things God's way does not always stop the opposition. Three local governors in the area of Israel balked at his arrival. Nehemiah knew without a doubt that God had given him the vision and opportunity to rebuild. But God did not make it easy for them to do what He called them to do.

- Nehemiah's enemies were political power brokers in the Trans-Jordan region who had the king's letter to them telling them to completely cooperate with Nehemiah. Yet the resentful politicians tried everything they could to stop the rebuilding of Jerusalem. Nehemiah did not back down. He was confident in his identity as God's servant. *Nehemiah 2:19-20*

RESPONDING TO FEAR TACTICS MEANT TO DISCOURAGE

- Fear is a normal human emotion designed by God to alert us to danger so we will take action against it. The proper response to fear is to take action against it. Nehemiah illustrates this for us as he dealt with every fear weapon of his enemies.

- **Weapon #1: Intimidation**—The enemies threatened physical attack. That did not discourage Nehemiah from doing what God had placed in his heart to do. He prayed and led the people in prayer for God to do His part in giving them protection. But they also did their part by posting guards day and night and carrying weapons with them while they worked. *Nehemiah 4:7-9,16-18*

- **Weapon #2: Distraction**—The enemies tried to distract Nehemiah from the work at hand and trap him in order to kill him. They thought Nehemiah would have been defenseless once out of Jerusalem and away from his army. But God gave Nehemiah wisdom to recognize the trap. *Nehemiah 6:2-4*

- **Weapon #3: Lies**—The enemies spread rumors about Nehemiah that that they were supposedly passing along to the king. Nehemiah called the news a lie and probably informed his boss, the king, that it was fake news. He recognized their fear tactics and turned to the one who could strengthen him for the work—God. *Nehemiah 6:5-9*

- **Weapon #4: Slander**—The enemies tried to use an insider to get Nehemiah to do wrong to save his life by shutting himself inside the temple even though he was not a priest and should not be inside the temple. But Nehemiah trusted God and obeyed God first. He recognized that Shemaiah was a false prophet hired by the enemies to intimidate Nehemiah and ruin his reputation with the Jews. *Nehemiah 6:10-13*

- **Weapon #5: Treason**—Some Jewish nobles were in cahoots with the bad guys through having intermarried with Nehemiah's political opponents. These nobles felt their power was also being threatened by Nehemiah. Disloyalty and treason are painful for any leader, especially a godly one who is serving God wholeheartedly. *Nehemiah 6:17-19*

TRUSTING GOD AS YOU RESPOND HIS WAY

- Opponents of Christ will use every weapon of discouragement to stop us from doing the work God has given us or to stop us from doing it well. We can be wise in how we respond to fake news and intimidation and all those other fear tactics.

  - ✓ Nehemiah needed **discernment** to recognize the error of those weapons and to avoid an improper response. We need that too.

  - ✓ Nehemiah needed God's **strength** to combat the weapons. He prayed, "Lord, strengthen my hands" (Nehemiah 6:9). We need to pray that too.

  - ✓ Nehemiah **trusted** in God while at the same time taking wise safety **precautions** (Nehemiah 4:16-23). We can do that in the wake of any news causing us fear.

Let Jesus satisfy your heart with complete trust in Him so that you will follow His way of living life instead of the world's way or your own way.

Lesson 9: Nehemiah 7-13

445-431 B.C.

DAY ONE STUDY

Ask the Lord Jesus to teach you through His Word.

For the ABC's of Nehemiah, see Lesson 8.

445 B.C.

Read Nehemiah 7:1-5.

1. What was challenging God's people?

2. What choices did they make or need to make?

3. What did God do or say to encourage them to trust Him and follow His way instead of the world's way or their own way?

4. How did the people respond?

Read Nehemiah 8:1-18. This took place 6 days after the wall was finished.

5. What was challenging God's people?

   • Verses 1-12—

   • Verses 13-18—

6. What choices did they make or need to make?

   • Verses 1-12—

   • Verses 13-18—

Focus on the Meaning: Not only did the leaders read the Word of God, but they also translated it from the Hebrew language into Aramaic, the common language of the Persian Empire. Some of the Jews present did not know Hebrew (13:24), having grown up in Babylon and elsewhere, away from Jews who maintained fluency in the Hebrew language. ... Ezra and his associates not only translated the Law, but they also explained what it meant and how it applied to the people. This is true Bible exposition. (*Dr. Constable's Notes on Nehemiah 2023 Edition*, pp. 46-47)

7. What did God do or say to encourage them to trust Him and follow His way instead of the world's way or their own way?

8. How did the people respond?

Application for today

9. Consider anything in this lesson that is similar to today. Find New Testament verses that you can apply in your life to that similar situation.

Your favorite verse(s) from today's study:

Respond to the Lord about what you learned today.

DAY TWO STUDY

Ask the Lord Jesus to teach you through His Word.

Read Nehemiah 9:1-38.

10. What was challenging God's people (vv. 1-3, 36-37)?

Focus on the Meaning: The people considered themselves slaves (of Persia) in God's land instead of recognizing that they were servants of God in His land. The Lord Almighty was superior to the Persian king and government. In reality, every person is a slave / servant to something—either a slave to sin or a servant to God (Romans 6:11-22). There is no other alternative.

11. What choices did they make or need to make?

12. What in the prayer of the Levite leaders (vv. 4-5) would have encouraged the people to trust God and follow His way instead of the world's way or their own way?

Scriptural Insight: This is one of the great prayers of the Old Testament. It praises God for His character and His faithfulness. It also reminds the listeners of their beginnings as a people and as a nation. In essence, it is remembering their spiritual "birth." Likewise, every Christian should remember their own spiritual birth with such fervency.

13. How did the people respond to the prayer?

Application for today

14. Consider anything in this lesson that is similar to today. Find New Testament verses that you can apply in your life to that similar situation.

Your favorite verse(s) from today's study:

Respond to the Lord about what you learned today.

DAY THREE STUDY

Ask the Lord Jesus to teach you through His Word.

Read Nehemiah 10:28-11:4 (first part).

15. What was challenging God's people?

16. What choices did they make or need to make?

17. How did the people respond (11:1-2)?

> *Optional reading:* Skim Nehemiah 11:4-12:26 to get details of everyday life for the Jews.

Read Nehemiah 12:27-13:3.

> **Historical Insight:** The mention of Darius the Persian in 12:22 probably refers to Darius II, the successor of Artaxerxes I. Darius ruled from 423-404 B.C. The text refers to an event that took place in Darius' reign (12:22). Therefore, Nehemiah must have written the book sometime after that reign began. (*Dr. Constable's Notes on Nehemiah 2022 Edition,* p. 2)

18. What grabbed your attention from vv. 27-43? See also Nehemiah 4:3.

19. What did God do or say to encourage them to trust Him and follow His way instead of the world's way or their own way?

20. How did the people respond (vv. 43-47)?

Scriptural Insight: Regarding Nehemiah 13:1-4, unbelieving immigrants from these nations were those denied full rights. This would explain why Rahab, a Canaanite, and Ruth, a Moabite, became citizens. They were both believers in Yahweh. (*Dr. Constable's Notes on Nehemiah 2023 Edition,* p. 61)

Application for today

21. Consider anything in this lesson that is similar to today. Find New Testament verses that you can apply in your life to that similar situation.

Your favorite verse(s) from today's study:

Respond to the Lord about what you learned today.

DAY FOUR STUDY

Ask the Lord Jesus to teach you through His Word.

Possibly 432-431 B.C.

Read Nehemiah 13:4-31.

After serving as governor for several years, Nehemiah returned to King Artaxerxes' service (v. 6) then came back some time later. The prophet Malachi reproved the Jews in Judah for the same sins that Nehemiah described in this chapter. You will see that in Lesson 10.

> **Think About It:** The words of Isaiah spoken 200 years before this time held true in Nehemiah's time. "When your judgments come upon the earth, the people of the world learn righteousness. But when grace is shown to the wicked, they do not learn righteousness; even in a land of uprightness they go on doing evil and do not regard the majesty of the Lord (Isaiah 26:9-10)." Sadly, this still holds true today.

22. What was challenging God's people?

- Verses 4-9—

- Verses 10-14—

- Verses 15-22—

- Verses 23-29—

> **Think About It:** Whom did Nehemiah leave in charge of Jerusalem during his absence? Perhaps Ezra died by this time. Obviously, the two trustworthy men overseeing Jerusalem (Nehemiah 7:2) were not leading at this time. Eliashib the priest was weak. Weak leaders do not inspire good things from the people. Sadly, many of the people forgot their oath to God when the strong man (Nehemiah) was gone.

23. What choices did Nehemiah make or need to make?

- Verses 4-9—

- Verses 10-14—

- Verses 15-22—

- Verses 23-30—

24. What did God do or say to encourage them to trust Him and follow His way instead of the world's way or their own way?

25. How did the people respond?

Application for today

26. Consider anything in this lesson that is similar to today. Find New Testament verses that you can apply in your life to that similar situation.

Your favorite verse(s) from today's study:

Respond to the Lord about what you learned today.

Recommended: Listen to the podcast "Nehemiah-Rebellious Hearts Spurn God's Grace" to reinforce what you have learned. Use the listener guide on the next page.

Nehemiah-Rebellious Hearts Spurn God's Grace

LISTENING ATTENTIVELY TO GOD'S WORD

- Six days after the wall was completed, all the people assembled together as one united group in a city square. Ezra read God's Law to them. They longed for God's Word enough that they were willing to listen attentively for 5-6 hours. Levites in the crowd explained to the meaning of what was read. This likely included some translation. *Nehemiah 8:2-3, 5-6*

- As they listened, the Jews began weeping. As a nation, they had failed to keep God's Law and suffered the consequences of their sin. But Nehemiah told them to experience God's joy instead and share their food with those who had nothing prepared. *Nehemiah 8:10*

- The people obeyed and finished this great gathering by celebrating the Feast of Booths. They experienced great joy because they finally understood the Law of God, their covenant with God, and how to be faithful to God through it. And while they were celebrating, they kept learning from God's Word for a whole week. *Nehemiah 8:12,18*

- God is a God of joy. When we seek Him and trust Him, He fills us with His joy. When we learn His Word and obey it, He fills us with His joy. When we go through times of weeping and sorrow, He fills us with His joy as we trust His goodness to us.

- God gave the Jews His land, laws that would make living in His land joyful, and His grace in every way so that as a people they could be successful. Why would anyone reject that?

  *When your judgments come upon the earth, the people of the world learn righteousness. But **when grace is shown to the wicked**, they **do not learn righteousness**; even in a land of uprightness they **go on doing evil** and **do not regard the majesty of the Lord**. (Isaiah 26:9b-10)*

- Through consequences of sinful behavior, people may learn what is right and wrong. But for those who have wicked hearts, they do not learn how to be righteous when they experience the grace of God. They ignore God's grace and His commands of how to live life His way. They find ways to keep doing evil.

REBELLIOUS HEARTS SPURN GOD'S GRACE

- A few days later, the people assembled in Jerusalem, confessed their sins, and were led in worship through a public prayer that reminded them of all the grace that God had shown them through the years in spite of their failures. Then, bound themselves by oath agreement to obey all God's commands. *Nehemiah 10:29*

- Just a few years later, Nehemiah left town for a couple of years. Some of the people forgot their oath to God, including the priests and leaders who lived in Jerusalem. The enemy Tobiah had been given a room in the temple courts in which to live! The sad truth is that rebellious hearts will always find ways to ignore or circumvent God's way of living life.

- We live in a world today that continually woos you away from serving God wholeheartedly. In fact, the culture encourages halfhearted obedience to God because it makes you feel good about yourself when you do good works. Rebellious hearts spurn God's grace. They want the blessings of God. But they do not want God!

FAITHFUL HEARTS ACT ON GOD'S BEHALF

- Nehemiah returned and took action on God's behalf. He walked right into that storeroom on the side of the temple and threw the man's stuff right out of the room. Then, he purified that room probably with lots of Lysol and restored it to its original purpose. He made it useful to God again. *Nehemiah 13:7-9*

- The people broke their covenant to provide for the Levites who were serving at the temple and leading them in worship at every assembly. Hungry Levites left Jerusalem to go back to their farms. Nehemiah rebuked the officials. These were the Levite leaders. He not only put them back to work to collect the tithes and offerings brought by the people, he selected two trustworthy men to be responsible for handing out the supplies to their fellow Levites. *Nehemiah 13:10-1*

- Nehemiah stopped the flagrant behavior of the merchants selling their wares in Jerusalem on the Sabbath by shutting and locking the gates for twenty-four hours. Those are intentional steps taken to end the abuse.

- To those who had married pagan women, he rebuked them and punished them in such a way they would never forget. Can you imagine the scene of him pulling out their hair? Then, he made them take an oath in God's name. I love his determination to honor God.

- Nehemiah did not put up with blatant sinful behavior by people who knew better. God's Word was readily available to them. They had likely heard it read just a few years earlier. Copies were evidently available. Yet, they chose to raise the high hand to God and not care what He thought.

EMBRACE GOD'S GRACE AND LEARN RIGHTEOUSNESS

- Do not do this, dear listener. If you have been spurning God's grace, confess your sin and choose to obey Him instead. Your God loves you greatly.

- When you follow His way, your life will be rewarded as you experience His love you. When you follow His way, you can trust His goodness working on your behalf. When you follow His way, He will fill your heart with joy. What the world has to offer will never measure up to that!

Let Jesus satisfy your heart with complete trust in Him so that you will follow His way of living life instead of the world's way or your own way.

Lesson 10: Malachi 1-4

432-430 B.C.

DAY ONE STUDY

ABC's of Malachi

Author

Malachi received its name from its author (Malachi 1:1). In Hebrew, the name comes from a word meaning "messenger," which points to Malachi's role as a prophet of the Lord, delivering God's message to God's people. We know nothing of Malachi's parentage, tribal roots, geographical origin, or other possible vocation. Like Habakkuk, the name Malachi occurs nowhere else in the Old Testament. All we know is that Malachi received and communicated the word of Yahweh to the Jews of his day. The New Testament quotes Malachi three times but does not reference him by name (Matthew 11:10; Mark 1:2; and Luke 7:27).

Malachi did not refer to any datable persons or events in his prophecy. So we must infer the date of writing from the text and traditional understandings of it. Malachi delivered his message of judgment to a Judean audience familiar with worshipping at the temple in Jerusalem (Malachi 2:11). He also used the Persian word for governor, indicating the time period when the Persian Empire ruled Israel. The prophet's concerns mirror those of Nehemiah's. Malachi perhaps wrote during the years that Nehemiah was away from Jerusalem (Nehemiah 13:6) or when he returned to face the mess that existed.

Background

During the 70 years of captivity, the Jews learned to trust in their God alone and give up any idolatrous tendencies. After the 70 years, the faithful were allowed to return to their homeland.

Ezra chapters 1-6 record the experiences of the exiles returning to their homeland (536 B.C.). Haggai and Zechariah ministered to those returnees in 520 B.C. and urged them to rebuild the temple. Events recorded in the Book of Esther took place in Persia between 483 and 473 B.C. A second group of about 5,000 Jews returned in 458 B.C. under Ezra's leadership. A revival among Jews took place after the return of the Jews to Israel and the rebuilding of the temple accompanied with lots of rejoicing.

Ezra instituted reforms to purify Israel's worship (Ezra chapters 7-10). A third group of Jews returned with Nehemiah in 444 B.C. His book describes what happened between 445 and 430 B.C., including the rebuilding of Jerusalem's walls. It is thought that Malachi ministered in Jerusalem during that period, perhaps between 432 and 431 B.C. while Nehemiah was away from Jerusalem. At the time of Malachi, the Israelites had been back in the land for more than a hundred years.

> **Historical Insight:** Life was not easy for the returnees during the ministry of this fifth-century B.C. restoration prophet. The people continued to live under Gentile (Persian) sovereignty even though they were back in their own land. Harvests were poor, and locust plagues were a recurring problem (3:11). ... Priests and people were still not observing the Mosaic Law as commanded, [regarding] sacrifices, tithes, and offerings. The Israelites still intermarried with Gentiles (2:11), and divorces were quite common (2:16). The spiritual, ethical, and moral tone of the nation was low. (*Dr. Constable's Notes on Malachi 2022 Edition,* pp. 5-6)

121

God sent Malachi to help them remember who they were and His goodness toward them, to recommit their lives to do life His way once again, and to restore the joy and blessing of living in His love.

Context

Malachi was one of the three postexilic writing prophets along with Haggai and Zechariah. His book is the twelfth and last book in the order of Minor Prophets (Hosea-Malachi).

Malachi's ministry marked the conclusion of the Old Testament direct revelation from God. For 400 years, there was silence until the birth of Jesus. God was not finished with His people, though. He still intervened and directed the history of Israel through that 400 years.

Ask the Lord Jesus to teach you through His Word.

Read Malachi chapter 1.

1. What was challenging God's people?

    - Verses 1-5—

    - Verses 6-14—

    Focus on the Meaning: Some of the people were bringing defective offerings to the Lord, and the priests were accepting those defective sacrifices. Both groups were guilty.

2. What choices did they make or need to make?

    - Verses 1-5—

    - Verses 6-14—

3. What did God do or say to encourage them to trust Him and follow His way instead of the world's way or their own way?

Application for today

4. Consider anything in this lesson that is similar to today. Find New Testament verses that you can apply in your life to that similar situation.

Your favorite verse(s) from today's study:

Respond to the Lord about what you learned today.

DAY TWO STUDY

Ask the Lord Jesus to teach you through His Word.

Read Malachi 2:1-16.

5. What was challenging God's people?

- Verses 1-9 (addressed to the priests)—

- Verses 10-16—

Scriptural Insight: The intermarriages with foreign (non-Jewish) women was a continual problem. See Ezra 9-10 and Nehemiah 13.

123

6. What choices did they make or need to make?

- Verses 1-9 (the priests)—

- Verses 10-16—

7. What did God do or say to encourage them to trust Him and follow His way instead of the world's way or their own way?

> **Think About It:** As the life of a community depends upon the keeper of its water supply to guard that supply from loss or contamination, so the life of Israel depended upon its priests to preserve God's written word and effectively to dispense it when '[people] should seek' it. (*Dr. Constable's Notes on Malachi 2023 Edition,* p. 37)

We do not know how the priests or the people responded to what God said to them.

Application for today

8. Consider anything in this lesson that is similar to today. Find New Testament verses that you can apply in your life to that similar situation.

Your favorite verse(s) from today's study:

Respond to the Lord about what you learned today.

DAY THREE STUDY

Ask the Lord Jesus to teach you through His Word.

Read Malachi 2:17-3:18.

9. What was challenging God's people?

    *   2:17-3:5—

    *   3:6-12—

    *   3:13-18—

Scriptural Insight: "Test me in this." The LORD had promised to bless the Israelites for obedience, so their obedience in bringing the full amount of tithes that the Law required would test (i.e., prove, demonstrate) His faithfulness to His promise. He promised to reward their full obedience with rain and harvests abundant enough to satisfy their needs. ... This verse has often been used to urge Christians to tithe. However, the New Covenant, under which Christians live, never specified the amount or percentage that we should give back to God out of what He has given to us. Rather it teaches that we should give regularly, sacrificially, as the LORD has prospered us, and joyfully (cf. 1 Cor. 16:2; 2 Cor. 8:1-4, 9-14; 2 Cor. 9:2, 7, 12; Phil. 4:10-19). In harmony with the principle of grace, ... the LORD leaves the amount that we give back to Him unspecified and up to us. Christians who sit under a steady diet of preaching that majors on God's grace often give far more than 10 percent, because they appreciate all that God has given them in Christ. (*Dr. Constable's Notes on Malachi 2022 Edition,* p. 55-56)

10. What choices did they make or need to make?

    *   2:17-3:5—

- 3:6-12—

- 3:13-18—

11. What did God do or say to encourage them to trust Him and follow His way instead of the world's way or their own way?

12. Write Malachi 3:16 in the space below.

> **Think About It:** What a contrast between these faithful God-worshipers and the neglectful priests (1:6-2:9), those who married outside of Judaism (2:10-16), and the arrogant who prosper yet challenge God (3:14-15)!

Application for today

13. Consider anything in this lesson that is similar to today. Find New Testament verses that you can apply in your life to that similar situation.

Your favorite verse(s) from today's study:

Respond to the Lord about what you learned today.

DAY FOUR STUDY

Ask the Lord Jesus to teach you through His Word.

Read Malachi chapter 4.

14. What did God do or say to encourage His people to trust Him and follow His way instead of the world's way or their own way?

15. How will the people respond to God's future messenger?

Application for today

16. Consider anything in this lesson that is similar to today. Find New Testament verses that you can apply in your life to that similar situation.

Your favorite verse(s) from today's study:

Respond to the Lord about what you learned today.

Recommended: Listen to the podcast "Malachi-Faithful Hearts Embrace God's Love" to reinforce what you have learned. Use the listener guide on the next page.

Malachi-Faithful Hearts Embrace God's Love

"I HAVE LOVED YOU"

- The Jewish people at the time of Malachi's messages were acting like we do today based on their appreciation or ignorance of God's great love for them—to embrace it or spurn it.

- Through Malachi, God declared first and foremost to them that He loves them. And He has loved them all the time of their existence, all the way back to their ancestor Jacob. So why were they questioning His love? *Malachi 1:2*

- The answer comes in Malachi chapters 1 and 2. God was not accepting their sacrifices. So they were not receiving His blessings. According to the Mosaic covenant, obedience to God's commands would bring great harvests, abundant rain, large families, and peace. God did not accept their sacrifices because they were spurning God's love for them and living life according to their own standards of what was okay—not His way.

- First, they were dishonoring God. Instead of bringing their best to Him, some of the people were bringing defective and diseased animals as offerings to God for sacrifices. And the priests were showing partiality in matters of the Law by accepting these filthy offerings and burning them on God's altar expecting God to be pleased. They were all cheating and thought they could get away with it.

- God reminded them of their purpose as priests and what they have chosen to do instead. As messengers of the Lord Almighty, they were to instruct the people how to respond in faithfulness to God's love by following God's way of living life. They chose to follow their own way instead and brought others with them. *Malachi 2:7-8)*

- The faithful Jews were watching this selfish, ungodly behavior of the priests and despised their ungodly behavior. Faithful hearts embrace God's love and want to follow His way. *Malachi 2:9*

- Besides being stingy, the Jews were not following God's way regarding marriage. God called it "breaking faith" with Him—being unfaithful. Some of them were marrying pagan women. Others were breaking their marriage covenants and divorcing their wives. God called this a violent action to the family. *Malachi 2:16b*

- Another way the rebellious hearts were rejecting God's love is by robbing God of what is already His. God asked them to trust Him with their security. They were in His land. He provided the crops that sustained them. The covenant promises were related not only to obedience but also to dependence on God more than on themselves. *Malachi 3:9-12; 2 Corinthians 8:1-5*

- The Jews were looking around and basically asking, "Is it really worth it to serve God and give sacrificially to Him? See all the rich people around us who care nothing for God and His love? Why should I follow your way instead of what the world tempts me to do to provide for myself and my future?" *Malachi 3:14-15*

FAITHFUL HEARTS EMBRACE GOD'S LOVE

- Some did not have rebellious hearts that were looking for ways to spurn God's love. And they joined together. These verses in Malachi chapter 3 are some of my favorite verses:

  *Then those who **feared the Lord talked with each other**, and **the Lord listened and heard**. A scroll of remembrance was written in his presence concerning those who feared the Lord and honored his name. "On the day when I act," says the Lord Almighty, "**they will be my treasured possession**. I will spare them, just as a father has compassion and spares his son who serves him. And **you will again see the distinction between the righteous and the wicked**, between those who serve God and those who do not. (Malachi 3:16-18)*

- God notices those whose hearts are faithful to Him—those who embrace His love for them. Faithful hearts talked with each other, sharing their concerns. The Lord listened and heard as they were talking. When we share our prayer needs with one another, we do not need to repeat them to God. He already heard them. That means we should have an awareness of His presence in our meetings. *Matthew 18:20*

- God answered by saying they are "my treasured possession." One day, there will be a visible distinction between those who serve God and those who do not. Faithful hearts as they embrace God's love choose the right side and should not be envious of the prosperous wicked and openly arrogant who seem to be getting away with their rebellion. The faithful ones will experience the joy of receiving righteousness and healing through faith in Christ. *Malachi 4:2; John 15:9-11*

- When you embrace God's love for you, you will keep His commands. You want to obey God because you are grateful for all that He has done for you. And Jesus fills you with joy, His joy, complete joy. Doesn't that make you want to kick up your heels?

Let Jesus satisfy your heart with complete trust in Him so that you will follow His way of living life instead of the world's way or your own way.

Lesson 11: Daniel 9-12

530 B.C. – End Times

DAY ONE STUDY

Ask the Lord Jesus to teach you through His Word.

In Daniel chapters 8-12, God revealed His prophetic plan for Israel during their time without a Davidic king through recorded visions and explanations of the visions. God also gave future promises to the whole world of His plan to provide an eternal kingdom to those who trust in Him.

> For the ABC's of Daniel, see Lesson 2.

539 B.C. Daniel was about 80 years old. **Read Daniel 9:1-19.**

1. What did Daniel know and do (vv. 1-3)?

2. For what did Daniel ask God (vv. 16-19)?

3. Consider what you have learned so far in this study, how did God answer this prayer?

Read Daniel 9:20-27.

4. What did God do or say in answer to Daniel's prayer?

Focus on the Meaning: The angel said that Daniel was "highly esteemed" in 9:23; 10:11, 19. Other translations say "greatly beloved" or "precious to God." Like Daniel, every Christian is also greatly beloved by God. See this truth in Ephesians 5:1 and Colossians 3:12. This is part of your **identity** in Christ.

5. What is the purpose for God's decree this time (v. 24)?

Focus on the Meaning: Seventy seven-year periods totals 490 years. As Jerusalem was suffering under the hand of Gentiles for 70 years (v. 2), so the Jews and Jerusalem would suffer under the hand of Gentiles for 490 years. "Your people" and "your holy city" are obvious references to the Jews and Jerusalem (cf. vv. 7, 11, 20). They do not refer to the church, which is a distinct entity from Israel (cf. 1 Cor. 10:32). ... The date 444 B.C., [Artaxerxes' decree to rebuild Jerusalem] then, probably marks the beginning of this 490-year period. Seven sevens plus sixty-two sevens equals 483 sevens or years. Gabriel predicted that after 483 years, Messiah would be cut off. Detailed chronological studies have been done that show that Jesus Christ's death occurred then. ... If one calculates the number of days involved in the Jewish and Babylonian calendar year, the year Messiah would be cut off comes out to A.D. 33. Several scholars have calculated that the day Jesus entered Jerusalem in His triumphal entry was precisely the last day of this long period. ... After it, the nation of Israel rejected Him. Whether or not the chronology is that exact, almost all conservative expositors agree that the death of Christ is in view and that it occurred at the end of the sixty-ninth week. (*Dr. Constable's Notes on Daniel 2022 Edition*, pp. 177, 179-180)

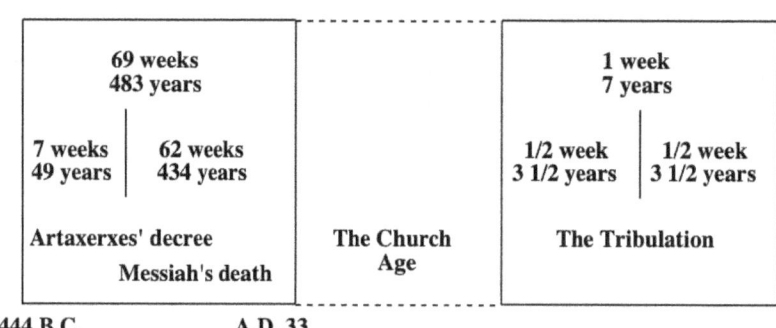

Daniel's Seventy Weeks
Dan. 9:24-27

(possible timeline taken from *Dr. Constable's Notes on Daniel 2022 Edition*, p. 185)

Application for today

6. What in this lesson encourages you?

Your favorite verse(s) from today's study:

Respond to the Lord about what you learned today.

DAY TWO STUDY

Ask the Lord Jesus to teach you through His Word.

537 B.C. Two years after the vision in Daniel 9.

Read Daniel 10:1-11:1.

7. What happened in verses 1-3?

8. After 3 weeks of waiting, what did Daniel see (vv. 4-7)?

9. What did Daniel experience (vv. 8-11)?

10. What did Daniel hear (vv. 12-14)?

Scriptural Insight: Michael (10:13, 21; 12:1; Jude 9) is one of only two angels that are identified in the Bible by name, the other being Gabriel (Daniel 9:21). Michael is a high-ranking angel who protects Israel. Some angels have more authority and power than others do (Ephesians 1:21). The man clothed in lined described in verses 5-6 must be an angel (see Daniel 12:7). Evidently the good angel who spoke to Daniel and touched him had performed some duty in Persia that involved the kings or rulers of that land. However, having received a commission from God to visit Daniel, he was not able to break away to deliver it because of the influence of the bad angel (prince of Persia) who exercised strong influence over Persia. Michael helped [the good angel] break away from this wicked angel's power so that he could visit Daniel. God's messenger had received help from Michael, so it seems unlikely that he was God Himself. (adapted from *Dr. Constable's Notes on Daniel 2023 Edition,* pp. 191-192)

11. How did Daniel respond (vv. 15-17)?

12. What happened next (10:18-11:1)?

Scriptural Insight: God does not open the door for human involvement in angelic warfare in the heavenly realms. No biblical instruction justifies any teaching that tells you to pray against and claim victory over certain demons by name. Michael's success was not due to Daniel's praying, for or against, certain angels or demons. However, we are given instruction about standing strong to face spiritual warfare against us (Ephesians 6:10-18). (adapted from *Dr. Constable's Notes on Daniel 2023 Edition,* pp. 193)

Application for today

13. What in this lesson encourages you?

Your favorite verse(s) from today's study:

Respond to the Lord about what you learned today.

Day Three Study

Ask the Lord Jesus to teach you through His Word.

Daniel 11 is a more detailed explanation of the vision revealed to Daniel fourteen years earlier recorded in Daniel 8 (Lesson 2, Day Two Study). The interpreting angel now explained the long-anticipated revelation about the future that involved Daniel's people, the Jews. The first part of this revelation concerns events preceding Messiah's first advent (vv. 2-35), and the second part concerns events preceding Messiah's second advent (11:36—12:4).

Read Daniel 11:2-35.

> **Historical Insight:** History has identified [the contemptible person in Daniel 11:21] as Antiochus IV (Epiphanes), the eighth king of the Seleucid dynasty. He ruled Syria from 175 to 164 B.C. ... Antiochus was especially vengeful against the Jews, whom he persecuted brutally. ... In one assault on Jerusalem, 40,000 Jews were killed in three days and 10,000 more were carried into captivity. This suppression came to a head in December 168 B.C., when Antiochus returned in frustration from Alexandria ... and vented his exasperation on the Jews. He sent his general, Apollonius, with twenty thousand troops under orders to seize Jerusalem on a Sabbath. There he erected an idol of Zeus and desecrated the altar by offering swine on it [in 168 B.C.]. This idol became known to the Jews as **'the abomination of desolation'**, which served as a type of a future abomination that will be set up in the Jerusalem sanctuary to be built in the last days (cf. Christ's prediction in Matt 24:15). Four years later, on December 25, 164 B.C., Judas Maccabaeus, a Jewish nationalist, led the Jews in rededicating the temple to Yahweh. This is the event that Jews have celebrated with Hanukkah ever since." (*Dr. Constable's Notes on Daniel 2022 Edition,* pp. 156-158)

14. What will the people who know their God do and receive (vv. 32-35)?

> **Historical Insight:** Antiochus' persecutions gave impetus to the Chassidim ("the Godly, Pious, Loyal Ones") movement that was already underway in Israel. The Chassidim advocated strict adherence to the Mosaic Law and the traditions of Judaism. Even today, the strictest orthodox Jews refer to themselves as Hasidim. The Maccabean revolt likewise fueled this movement since it was a political and military manifestation of the Chassidim conservative philosophy. The Chassidim movement really resulted in the

spiritual survival of Israel until Jesus' time. Some of the Chassidim became the sect of the Pharisees ("Separated Ones"), which appears in the Gospels. Later a smaller group of Chassidim became the isolationist Essene community that lived at Qumran beside the Dead Sea. The Essenes repudiated the rationalism of the Sadducees and the materialism of the Pharisees. All these groups had their roots in **"the people who know their God"** (v. 32). (*Dr. Constable's Notes on Daniel 2022 Edition*, pp. 210-211)

Application for today

15. Each of the 100 specific prophecies delivered to Daniel in vv. 2-35 literally came true as promised within a few hundred years of Daniel recording them. How does knowing this encourage you about the future return of Christ?

Your favorite verse(s) from today's study:

Respond to the Lord about what you learned today.

DAY FOUR STUDY

Read Daniel 11:36-45.

In this part of chapter 11, the angel's vision refers to the Antichrist who will appear in the distant future, also described in Daniel 9:26-27. This section of Daniel 11 continues in Daniel 12.

16. What do you learn about this future antichrist?

Read Daniel chapter 12.

17. What are the promises to God's people (vv. 1-3)?

Scriptural Insight: The angel meant a physical resurrection, rather than just a renewal of the soul. This seems clear since he specified that they will arise from "the dust of the ground." For more Old Testament verses that predicted the resurrection of the body, see Job 19:25-27 (not a Jew), Isaiah 26:19 (all believers), Isaiah 53:11 (the Messiah); Hosea 6:2 (raised in 3 days), Jonah 1:17 (3 days as a sign of the Messiah), and Psalm 16:9-11 (the Messiah and believers).

18. What happened next?

- Verses 4-7—

- Verses 8-12—

Scriptural Insight: The LORD measured the time between the end, presumably the end of the Tribulation, and the time that the Antichrist will terminate Jewish sacrifices and desecrate the temple (cf. Matt. 24:15). It will be 1,290 days. This is 30 days longer than the three and one-half years previously mentioned (v. 7; cf. 7:25; Rev. 11:2; 12:6, 14; 13:5). Consequently, the extra month must involve time before the three and one-half years, after it, or both. (*Dr. Constable's Notes on Daniel 2022 Edition*, p. 226)

19. What is the promise to Daniel in verse 13?

Application for today

20. How do Daniel 12:2 and Daniel 12:13 relate to your life as a Christian?

21. How does Daniel 12:10 encourage you?

Your favorite verse(s) from today's study:

Read the next section and answer the question that follows it.

GOD'S STEADFAST LOVE WORKED FOR OUR FUTURE

As bad as the destruction of Jerusalem and the temple looked, God caused it to work for good for His people, that eventually benefited you and me. He had a greater purpose than purifying His people. Those 400 years of silence regarding any written or spoken words directly from God were not without God actively working on behalf of the Jews and eventually us.

Politically

After the exile, Israel ceased to be an independent nation and became a minor territory in a succession of larger empires—Babylonian, Persian, Greek, and Roman (Daniel 2 vision). The rulers were often ruthless against the Jews and continually tried to force idolatry on the Jewish people.

In the century before Jesus was born, Rome conquered Israel and the rest of the countries surrounding the Mediterranean. The Roman general Pompey in his conquest of Jerusalem massacred priests in the performance of their duties and entered the Most Holy Place. This sacrilege began Roman rule in a way that Jews could neither forgive nor forget! Herod, a non-Jew, was appointed king over Israel by the Roman Senate in 40 B.C. But he was still subject to Rome.

Yet, the Romans brought good things to the Mediterranean lands. They brought "peace" to the whole region, although it was a forced peace. Law and order prevailed. Anyone who rebelled was quickly squashed by the powerful Roman army.

And the Romans poured a lot of effort into major construction of magnificent buildings as well as a system of roads so people could travel from the farthest reaches of the Empire back to mother Rome. This made travel and communication between towns much easier along those roadways. Paul and the other missionaries of the first century utilized those roads for their travel as well as the many shipping options available to them for sea travel.

Through the activity of the Romans, God was at work in the background to prepare the way for answering the prayers of all people for deliverance. Part of His work was to provide the environment in which His Son Jesus would be born and live.

Culturally

Alexander the Great was the Greek king who conquered lots of territory from Greece eastward. Daniel prophesied about this in Daniel chapters 2, 7, and 8. This action of expanding the Greek Empire spread the Greek language and culture to all those conquered nations. For the next 200 years after Alexander's conquests, just about everyone in the Mediterranean world learned to speak and write Greek. And all the ancient documents were translated into Greek including the Old Testament around the year 250 B.C. This Greek version of the Old Testament scriptures is called "The Septuagint" from the Latin word for "seventy" because it was reportedly prepared by 70 scholars in 70 days. By the time of Jesus, most of those people meeting in synagogues around the Mediterranean Sea were using the Septuagint as their Scriptures.

Paul and other New Testament writers wrote in Greek which could be read everywhere in those countries influenced by the Greek culture. Through the spread of the Greek empire, God was at work in the background to prepare the way for answering the prayers of His people for deliverance. Part of His work included a common language.

Religiously

During the exile from their homeland (605-538 B.C.), the Jews living in Babylonian territory (modern Iraq) were cut off from the temple, stripped of their nationhood, and surrounded by pagan religious practices. They could not depend on those travels to Jerusalem for festivals and sacrifices a few times a year to satisfy their spiritual needs. In their places of exile, though, they carried their scriptures with them, especially the first five books of the Old Testament called the Torah. They kept their identity as God's people and learned how to live out their faith through personal piety and prayer rather than the sacrifices that were no longer available to them.

THE SYNAGOGUE

The Jews met together in community groups for worship and reading of their Scriptures. This new center of worship became the local synagogue (similar to a church community). As a result, Judaism became a faith that could be practiced wherever the Jews could meet and the Torah could be read.

The synagogue meetings gave rise to a new class of professional clergy within Judaism—the rabbi. The rabbi was both a scholar and a teacher tasked with explaining God's expectations to the common people. Early rabbis compiled a series of teachings (the Talmud) that further explain the Torah. These were oral teachings adopted by the scribes and Pharisees and included additional laws that kept the focus on Jewish purity as well as piety. Jesus referred to these as the oral "traditions." The oral traditions were recorded around 200 A.D.

THE DIASPORA

The dispersion of Israel that began with the exile accelerated during the years that followed so that by the time of Jesus, Jews filled every land in the Middle East. Those Jews living outside of the land of Israel were called the Diaspora. For almost seven centuries, Jews came to Jerusalem to participate in the worship, sacrifices, and other activities carried on at the temple. Back home, they concentrated their religious life in the study of the Scriptures and the life of the synagogue wherever Jewish communities existed. This helped to preserve Judaism but also prepared the way for the Christian gospel.

The missionaries of the early church began their outreach ministries among the Diaspora in their synagogues, using the Greek translation of the Old Testament. Within many Jewish synagogue congregations were "God-fearing" Gentiles —the non-Jews who believed in the Jewish God and followed the Law to some extent but not fully.

God had the bigger picture. He turned something that looked bad into something that was great for not only the Jews but also for Gentiles throughout the Persian, Greek, and Roman Empires. God is so good in everything He does!

THE PHARISEES

During the time period after the exile, a religious group formed to keep Israel pure from idolatry. They did this by insisting that keeping the Law was the only way that the Jews would be able to live righteously before God in a world that had changed drastically since the days of Moses. We know them in the Gospels as the Pharisees. Even though they had become petty and legalistic by the time of Jesus, they had helped to make sure Israel never again turned to idols thus purifying it for the coming of Jesus Christ. Though few in number, they enjoyed the support of the people and were the only party to survive the destruction of the temple in A.D. 70, thus being the spiritual progenitors of modern Judaism.

God's Plan

God's steadfast love brought back a remnant of faithful Jews to regain their land and their purpose to once again be a light for the Gentiles. Israel would never again participate in the idolatry and worship of false gods of the surrounding nations. Israel clung to their God for the next few hundred years, thus preparing the Jews for the coming of their Messiah. I would have given up on such a stiff-necked people. God did not. Thankfully in His steadfast love, He is still wooing those whose hearts are pliable towards Him.

> **Scriptural Insight:** Because God is a God of order, He deals with us in orderly ways. He sent His Son, Jesus Christ, into the world at just the right time (Galatians 4:4). He prefaced the arrival of Jesus with nearly [four] thousand years of a sacrificial pattern designed to teach people about holiness and repentance (Leviticus 4:35). Through the Hebrew nation, He gave His law and showed us what was required to approach a holy God (Exodus 19:12; Leviticus 17:11). By the time Jesus came, the Jewish people were well-schooled in the sacrificial system and [should have] understood their need for a Messiah to make them right with God (Zechariah 9:9; Hebrews 9:22–23). God did not spring the idea of a Savior on the world. He spent centuries patiently preparing the world in an orderly fashion (Mark 14:49; John 3:16–18; 5:39). (S. Michael Houdmann, *"What does it mean that God is a God of order,"* gotquestions.org)

STICKING TO YOUR FAITH

When Jesus came to earth, the power of God's presence was manifested in a very personal way. As Bible teacher Tony Evans says, "Jesus is God's selfie." Jesus said, "Anyone who has seen Me has seen the Father" (John 14:9). He lived His life in dependence on God so that we would know how to do that too. Jesus gave His life for us on the cross so that we could become new creatures with complete forgiveness of our sins and a reconciled relationship with our God. Jesus rose from the dead so that He could give His life to us through the Holy Spirit that lives inside every believer. When we are willing, Jesus can live His life through us.

Christian, take the truths of Scripture to heart. Remember who you are and the wonderful things God has done for you through your faith in His Son Jesus Christ. If you have been pulled away from God by the world's destructive influences, say "NO" to those destructive influences. Recommit to doing life God's way rather than the world's way or your own way. Stick to your faith, and enjoy the blessings of belonging to God and living obediently to Him.

22. What did you learn from this section about the work of God to prepare the way for His Son Jesus Christ to come to earth?

Respond to the Lord about what you learned today.

Recommended: Listen to the podcast "Daniel-Rest Then Rise to Receive Your Inheritance" to reinforce what you have learned. Use the listener guide on the next page.

Daniel-Rest Then Rise to Receive Your Inheritance

GOD'S PLAN AND PREPARATION

- Trying to understand all the prophecies about the end times is like having a bunch of puzzle pieces that look similar but without the picture on the box top to tell you how to arrange them. All we know for sure are the border pieces.

    Border piece #1: The Rapture of the Saints. One day, Jesus Christ will appear as Savior to gather His own together in the clouds. All those who are in Christ, dead and alive, will receive resurrection bodies immediately as they meet Christ in the air. *1 Thessalonians 4:13-17*

    Border piece #2: The Great Tribulation. This is the time when God's wrath against sin is directed toward earth. According to Daniel chapter 9, this is the 70th week so it will last seven years. We Christians up to the time of the Rapture will not be on earth. We are saved from the wrath of God. We will not endure it. And God will make it happen just as He says. *1 Thessalonians 5:2-3; Revelation chapters 4-19*

    Border piece #3: The Antichrist. A ruthless leader will proclaim himself first as a peacemaker then break his promise in the middle of the seven years. It is pointless to try to figure out who the Antichrist is since he will not be revealed until after the Rapture. *Daniel 9:27; 2 Thessalonians 2:6-8*

    Border piece #4: Christ and the Kingdom. Christ will return back to earth to exact justice against unbelievers and set up His kingdom on earth. *2 Thessalonians 1:8-10; Revelation 19-20*

- Obsessing on end times prophecy is a waste of time. The words are rolled up and sealed until it is time for God to act. While waiting, we can saturate our minds with what has already been fulfilled and what is promised to us personally. *Daniel 12:9-10*

THE EXPECTATION OF RESURRECTION

- Many Old Testament passages prophesied the resurrection of the body. *Daniel 12:2; Job 19:25-27; Psalm 16:9-10; Isaiah 26:19*

- Most of the Jewish people believed their bodies would rise from the grave and be made new. They just did not expect this of their Messiah.

THE EXPECTATION OF THE MESSIAH

- The Jews of Jesus' day believed that when the Messiah comes, God would begin a new age—His kingdom—first by resurrecting and judging all the dead, then giving the Holy Spirit to the righteous, and finally righting all the wrongs on planet Earth. The Messiah would reign as king over the whole earth from Jerusalem. They just did not know that God's plan would be a two-stage process.

- But the Old Testament predicted the Messiah would die and be resurrected from the grave on the third day. Jesus claimed that about Himself as He taught His disciples. *Mark 8:31; Isaiah 53:10-11; Jonah 1:17; Hosea 6:2*

- When the early Christians spoke of Jesus being raised from the dead, they were claiming that something happened to Jesus which had never happened to anyone else—yet. The resurrection declared that what Jesus did in His life and in His death was the work of God's son—the Messiah Because of Jesus' finished work on the cross, God could give His Spirit to faithful believers.

UNTIL HE COMES

- Jesus was taken up to heaven before witnesses in a cloud of glory. Two angels declared to His followers that He would return in the same way—bodily and visibly. UNTIL then, He waits as king in His glorified human body UNTIL the Father says it is time to return in the same way to set up His earthly kingdom. We are living in this UNTIL time. *Acts 3:20-21*

- The Bible says that creation is groaning in pain because of sin and God's curse on it. God will restore His creation to its initial glory. The Resurrection began the process.

- Until the time comes for God to restore everything, we are waiting. This UNTIL time (also called the "time of the Gentiles") will last until the fullness of the Gentiles is reached. The Rapture of the believers is the signal that the time of God's grace to the Gentiles ends.

TRUTH FOR NOW

What We Can Know for Sure: Jesus is coming back to gather His own, and not one believer is going to miss it—whether you are dead, sleeping in your bed, or taking a shower. You will not miss His coming. Isn't that good news? We just do not know when He is returning.

What We Can Know for Sure: Jesus said conditions on this planet are not going to get better but worse! We can forget the whole idea of world peace until He comes back. Although believers are encouraged to individually live in peace with each other and with unbelievers, we humans can never bring about world peace. Only Jesus as king on earth can. *Mark 13:7-8*

What We Can Know for Sure: Jesus described a great time of worldwide, massive tribulation. This Great Tribulation has not happened yet. The destruction of Jerusalem in 70 A.D. was not the worst that had happened before that or even since that time. It is still to come, dear listener. *Mark 13:14-23*

What We Can Know for Sure: Jesus is returning to planet Earth with His angels and saints to defeat the evil forces against Him and set up His Kingdom in Jerusalem. We live in a world of people who are at war with God. The war will continue in this direction until the King ends it, which He will do. *Revelation 19-20*

> *"As for you, go your way till the end. You will **rest**, and then at the end of the days you will **rise** to **receive** your allotted inheritance." (Daniel 12:13)*

Let Jesus satisfy your heart with complete trust in Him so that you will follow His way of living life instead of the world's way or your own way.

Map of Babylonian / Persian Empires

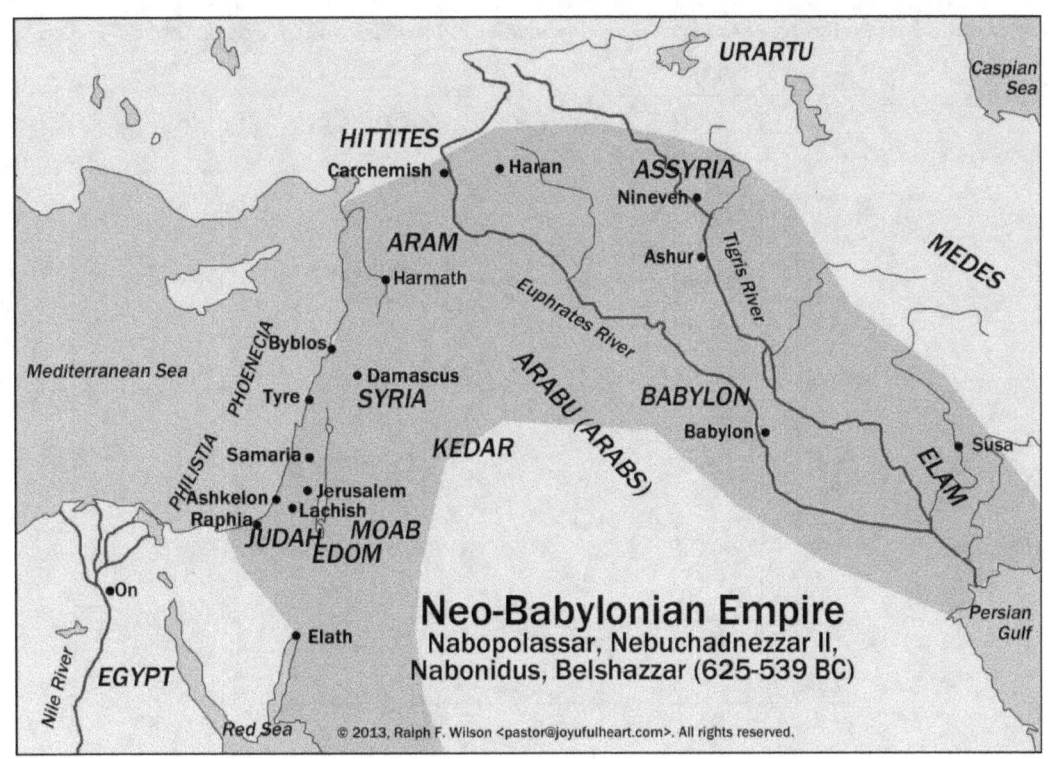

(Map above accessed at sturgiswesthistory.weebly.com.)

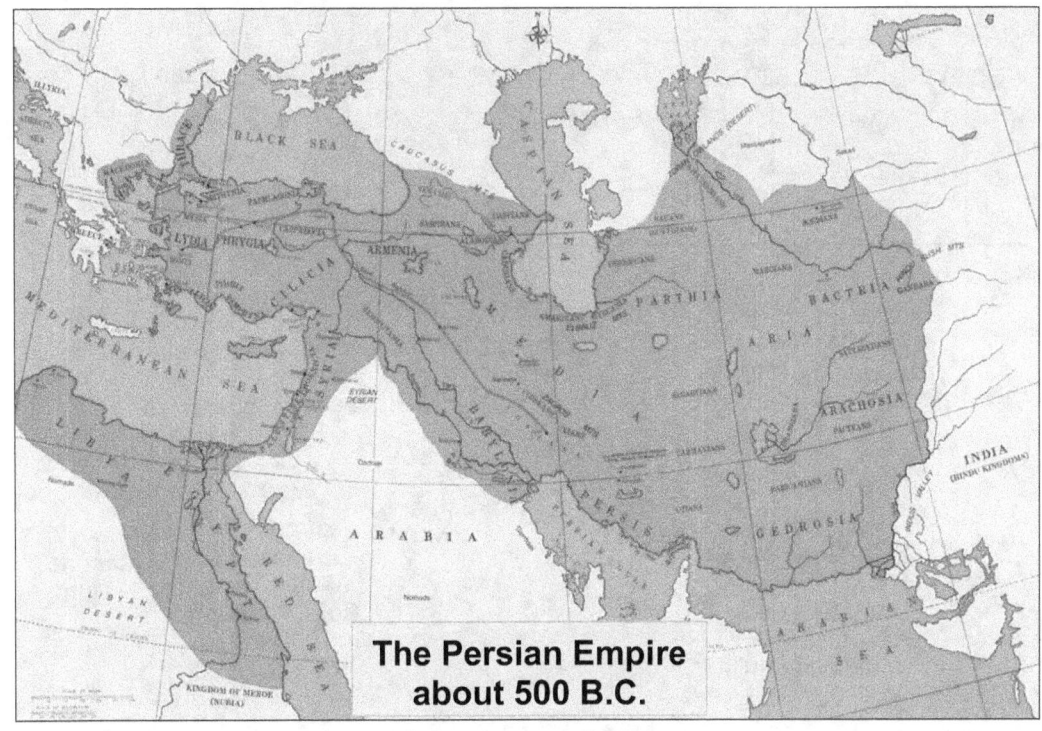

(Map above accessed at reddit.com)

Chronological Charts of Post-Exilic Books and Events

(Charts on this page are from *Dr. Constable's Notes on Ezra 2022 Edition,* pp. 6-7)

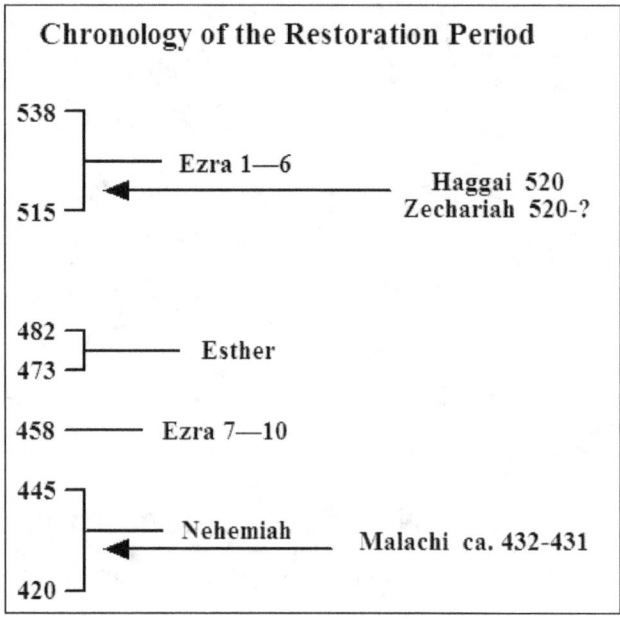

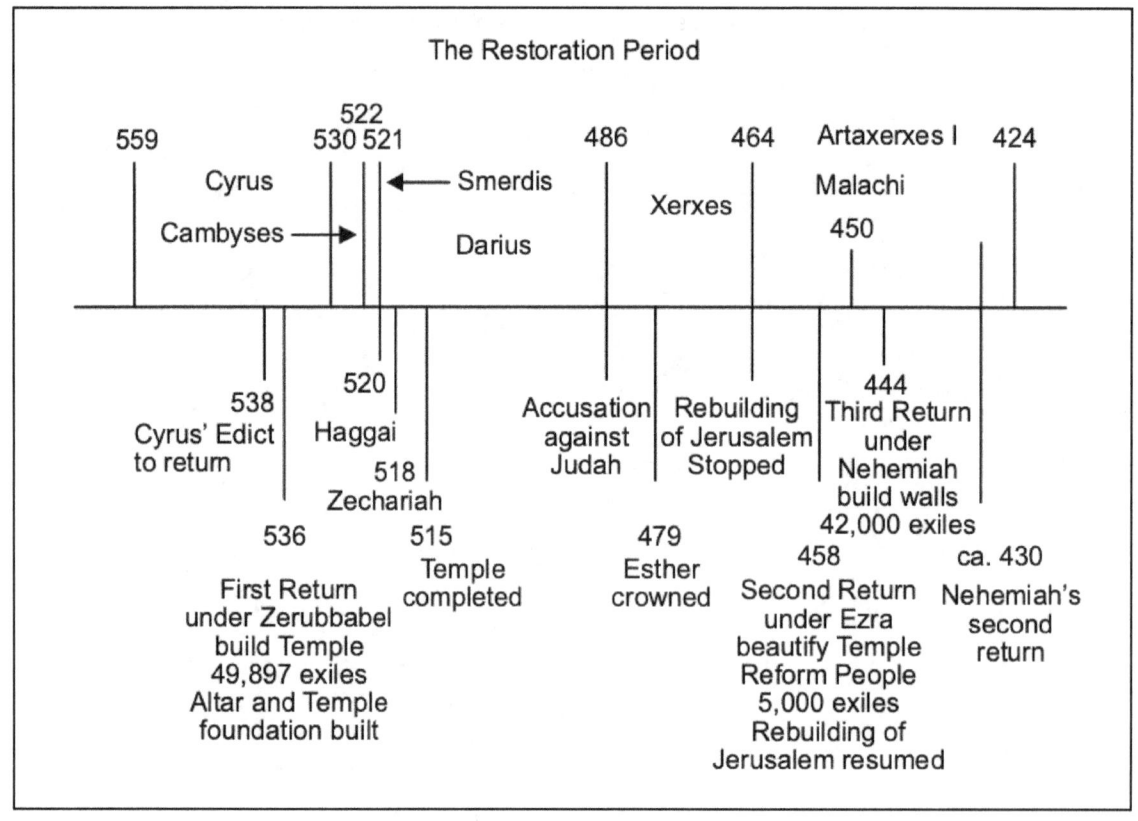

EVENTS AND REFERENCES

(Chart on this page from *Dr. Constable's Notes on Zechariah 2022 Edition*, pp. 5-6)

Event	Date	Book
Cyrus issued his edict allowing the Jews to return home.	538 B.C.	Ezra 1
About 50,000 Jews returned with Zerubbabel and Joshua.	536 B.C.	Ezra 2; Neh. 7
The altar was rebuilt and sacrifices resumed.	536 B.C.	
Work on the temple began but then halted.	536 B.C.	Ezra 3:1-4
The Jews were occupied with rebuilding their own homes.	536-522 B.C.	Hag. 1—2
Cyrus died; his son, Cambyses II, succeeded him as ruler.	530-522 B.C.	
Smerdis ruled Persia.	522 B.C.	
Darius the Great rules Persia.	522-486 B.C.	
Darius confirmed Cyrus' decree and encouraged the Jews to continue rebuilding the temple.	520 B.C.	Ezra 6:1-14
Haggai preached his first three sermons.	520 B.C., 6th - 7th months	Hag. 1:1, 15; 2:1
Zechariah preached his first sermon.	520 B.C., 8th month	Zech. 1:1
Haggai preached his fourth and fifth sermons.	520 B.C., 9th month	Hag. 2:10, 20
Zechariah received his eight night visions.	520 B.C., 11th month	Zech. 1:7
Joshua, the high priest, was crowned.	520 B.C., 11th month	Zech. 6:9-15
The delegation from Bethel arrived, and Zechariah preached again.	518 B.C., 9th month	Zech. 7:1
The Jews completed the temple and dedicated it.	515 B.C., 12th month	Ezra 6:15
Xerxes I (Ahasuerus) reigned over Persia.	486-464 B.C.	Esth. 2:16
Artaxerxes I reigned over Persia.	464-424 B.C.	
About 5,000 Jews returned to Palestine under Ezra's leadership.	458 B.C.	Ezra 7:7
Artaxerxes I sent Nehemiah to rebuild Jerusalem's walls.	445 B.C.	Neh. 2:1
Nehemiah led the third return to Palestine.	444 B.C.	Neh. 2:9
Malachi ministered.	432-431 B.C.	

Small Group Discussion Guide

The following guide is designed for groups that meet for about 1½ hours or less. You will notice that some questions are skipped for the sake of time.

Tell them how to find the podcasts (melanienewton.com/podcasts or any podcast platform— search "Satisfied" by Melanie Newton, Season 18). Or you can read the blogs associated with the podcasts at melanienewton.com/blog. Choose Ezra to Malachi category then scroll to find the title you want.

INTRODUCTION

Start with prayer.

Get acquainted with each other. Ask a general question or two such as, "Share your name, where you live, and one thing you would like the group to know about you."

Introduce the study

- Who has good knowledge of Old Testament history? There is an Old Testament Summary and Timeline on page 2. There are two maps at the end of the book that will help you during the study to get your geographic bearings. Also a couple of timeline charts.

- God is the same God in the Old Testament and New Testament. He extended grace and mercy to people in the Old Testament. People received eternal life by faith in God. For Jews, their earthly life was managed by the Mosaic Law given to Israel. Its purpose was to lead people to faith in God, devotion to God, and a relationship with God.

- Look at Contents page. We will cover these books but not everything in them. Real people. Real events.

- Walk through the Introduction (pages 1-3 including Discussion Guidelines. Point out maps and charts at the end of the study.

Why Study the Old Testament:

- Look at Lesson One. Read the verses in Qs1-4 and discuss the questions.

- We will not be focusing on historical information as much as what we can learn about endurance, encouragement, teaching, rebuking, correcting, training in righteousness so we might have HOPE in our present world.

Simple Things to Know When Studying the Old Testament

- Read this section in Lesson One and ask what grabbed their attention from it (Q5)?

In this study, we will look at how to flourish in a pagan world and stick to our faith in God. We will also see the two aspects of trusting God: 1) Trust God as you do your part His way; 2) Trust God to do His part alongside what you are doing. God knows exactly what we are going through today in your world because He has been through it before with Israel! And His solutions have not changed. This study of Daniel, Ezra, Nehemiah, Esther, Haggai, Zechariah, and Malachi will help Old Testament history come alive for you.

> **Recommendation:** Listen to a worship song such as "One Pure and Holy Passion," which fits very well with this study.

LESSON 1: JEREMIAH AND EZEKIEL TO THE EXILES

Each lesson in this study covers several chapters. Choose ahead of time which verses from the questions the group will read aloud as you proceed through the discussion. My recommendations are below.

Get acquainted: What is your current job or your last job if you are retired? Hint: avoid job history!

Start with prayer.

The Introduction Podcast:

- Listen together or before meeting. Ask what grabbed their attention.

Day One

- Qs 1-5 if you did not do this in your first meeting.
- Ask what grabbed their attention from the Historical Background (Q6). Discuss Q7.

Day Two

- Ask if anything grabbed their attention from the ABC's of Jeremiah.
- Read Jeremiah 24:4-7. Ask Q8.
- Read Jeremiah 29:1-7 from book. Ask Q9.
- Read Jeremiah 29:8-9. Ask Q10.
- Read Jeremiah 29:10-14. Ask Qs 11-14. Read Jeremiah 9:23-24 in book.
- Read Jeremiah 44:15-19. Ask Qs 15&16.
- Read Jeremiah 44:23-29. Ask Qs 17-19.
- Discuss Q20. Ask for their favorite verses.

Day Three

- Ask if anything grabbed their attention from the ABC's of Ezekiel.
- Read Ezekiel 11:16-21. Ask Qs 21-23. Read the paragraph that follows Q23.
- Ask Q24 (skip reading the verses). Read "Focus on the Meaning."
- Read Ezekiel 13:17-19. Ask Qs 25-26. Read "Focus on the Meaning."
- Read Ezekiel 13:20-23. Ask Q27.
- Discuss Q28. Ask for their favorite verses.

Day Four

- Read both passages and ask Qs 29-31.

Other

- Discuss the podcast.
- Pray

> **Recommendation:** Listen to a worship song such as "One Pure and Holy Passion," which fits very well with this study.

LESSON 2: DANIEL 1-8

This lesson covers several chapters. Choose ahead of time which verses from the questions the group will read aloud as you proceed through the discussion. My recommendations are below.

Start with prayer.

Day One

- What grabbed their attention from the ABC's of Daniel? Emphasize the last sentence in the "Context" section.
- Read Daniel 1:1-2. Qs 1 & 2. Read "Dependent Living."
- Read Daniel 1:15-21. Qs 3-5.

Day Two

- Read Daniel 2:1-3, 10-13. Q6.
- Read Daniel 2:14-18. Q7.
- Q8—Read the verses for each section and answer the question.
- Skip the chart. Read Daniel 7:9-10. Q9.
- Read Daniel 7:13-14 and Matthew 26:64. Q10.
- Read Daniel 7:18, 26-27. Q11. Read the "Scriptural Insight."

Day Three

- Q12.
- Read Daniel 3:13-18. Q13.
- Read Daniel 3:24-30. Qs 14-15.
- Qs16 & 17. Read verses in Q17.
- Qs18-20.

Day Four

- Qs21 & 22.
- Read Daniel 5:21-24. Qs 23 & 24.
- Read Daniel 6:3-5. Q25.
- Read Daniel 6:10-11. Q26.
- Read Daniel 6:17-23. Q27.
- Read Daniel 6:25-28. Qs 28 & 29.

Other

- Discuss the podcast.
- Pray

Recommendation: Listen to a worship song such as "You Are God Alone," by Phillips, Craig, & Dean, which fits very well with this study.

LESSON 3: EZRA 1:1-5:2; HAGGAI 1-2

This lesson covers several chapters. Choose ahead of time which verses from the questions the group will read aloud as you proceed through the discussion. My recommendations are below.

Start with prayer.

Day One

- What grabbed their attention from the ABC's of Ezra?
- Read Ezra 1:1-8,11 Q1 and "Historical Insight."
- Skip reading Ezra 2. Qs 2&3.
- Read Psalm 137:1-6. Q4.
- Read Psalm 126. Q5.
- Discuss Qs 6&7 (read the verses). Q7 can be shared in small groups of 2-3 for 5 minutes.

Day Two

- Read Ezra 3:1-4,10-13. Qs8-11.
- Read Ezra 4:1-5, 24. Qs 12&13. Read paragraph following Q13.
- Q14.
- Discuss Q15.

Day Three

- What grabbed their attention from the ABC's of Haggai?
- Read Ezra 5:1-2 and Haggai 1:2-9. Read "From the Hebrew."
- Qs 16-18. Read "Think About It."
- Read Haggai 1:12-14. Q19.
- Discuss Q20. This would be good for a breakout session.
- Skip Q21. Ask for their favorite verses.

Day Four

- Read Haggai 2:1-9. Qs 22&23.
- Read Haggai 2:18-23. Q24.
- Discuss Q25.
- Ask for their favorite verses.

Other

- Discuss the podcast.
- Pray

> **Recommendation:** Listen to a worship song such as "Lord, I Need You," which fits very well with this study.

LESSON 4: ZECHARIAH 1-8

This lesson covers several chapters. Choose ahead of time which verses from the questions the group will read aloud as you proceed through the discussion. My recommendations are below.

Start with prayer.

Day One

- What grabbed their attention from the ABC's of Zechariah?
- Read Zechariah 1:1-6 and "From the Hebrew." Q1.
- Read Zechariah 1:13-17. Q2.
- Read Zechariah 2:4-8 then 10-13. Q3.
- Q4. Ask for their favorite verses.

Day Two

- Read "Scriptural Insight" then Zechariah 3:1-10. Q5.
- Q6 (do not read verses).
- Read Zechariah 6:9-15. Qs7-9.
- Read Zechariah 4:6-10. Q10.
- Q11. Ask for their favorite verses.

Day Three

- Read Zechariah 7:1-2. Q12.
- Read Zechariah 7:7-10. Q13 and "Scriptural Insight."
- Q14.
- Q15. This would be good for a small group breakout session.

Day Four

- Read Zechariah 8:1-6. Q16.
- Read Zechariah 8:7-9, 13. Q17.
- Read Zechariah 8:15-19. Q18.
- Read Zechariah 8:20-23. Qs19-20.

Other

- Discuss the podcast.
- Pray

Recommendation: Listen to a worship song such as "What a Beautiful Name It Is," which fits very well with this study.

LESSON 5: EZRA 5-6; ZECHARIAH 9-14

This lesson covers several chapters. Choose ahead of time which verses from the questions the group will read aloud as you proceed through the discussion. My recommendations are below.

Start with prayer.

Day One

- As what grabbed their attention from the Historical Insight?
- Read Ezra 5:1-5, 11, 17. Qs1-3.
- Read Ezra 6:1-13, 22. Qs4&5.
- Q6. Read verses for each section.
- Discuss Q7. Ask for their favorite verses.

Day Two

- Read Zechariah 9:9-12. Q8.
- Skip reading verses. Ask Q9.
- Read Zechariah 10:1-3. Q10.
- Q11. Read verses for each section.
- Discuss Q12. Ask for their favorite verses.

Day Three

- Q13. Read verses for each section.
- Read Zechariah 12:10-14. Q14.
- Q16. Skip reading verses.
- Read Zechariah 13:7-9. Q16.
- Discuss Q17. Ask for their favorite verses.

Day Four

- Q18. Read verses for each section.
- Discuss Q19. Read "Focus on the Meaning."
- Discuss Q20. Ask for their favorite verses

Other

- Discuss the podcast.
- Pray

Recommendation: Listen to a worship song such as "You Are God Alone," which fits very well with this study.

LESSON 6: ESTHER

This lesson covers several chapters. Choose ahead of time which verses from the questions the group will read aloud as you proceed through the discussion. My recommendations are below.

Start with prayer.

Day One

- What grabbed their attention from the ABC's of Zechariah?
- Q1. Do not read verses.
- Read Esther 2:5-11, 15-17. Qs2&3.
- Read Esther 2:21-23. Q4.
- Q5. Ask for their favorite verses.

Day Two

- Read Esther 3:1-4. Qs6&7.
- Read Esther 4:9-17. Q8.
- Read Esther 5:1-8. Q9.
- Q10. This would be a good small group breakout question.
- Q11. Ask for their favorite verses.

Day Three

- Read Esther 6:1-3, 10-11. Qs12&13.
- Read Esther 7:1-6. Qs14&15.
- Read Esther 8:1-8, 16-17. Qs16&17.
- Q18. Ask for their favorite verses.

Day Four

- Read Esther 9:29-32. Qs19-21.
- Read Esther 10:1-3. Q22.
- Read 1 Peter 5:6-7. Q23.
- Q24

Other

- Discuss the podcast.
- Pray

Recommendation: Listen to a worship song such as "The Great I Am," which fits very well with this study.

LESSON 7: EZRA 7-10

This lesson covers several chapters. Choose ahead of time which verses from the questions the group will read aloud as you proceed through the discussion. My recommendations are below.

Start with prayer.

Day One

- Review what has happened so far in Ezra.
- Read Ezra 7:6-11. Q1.
- Read Ezra 7:12-26. Qs2&3.
- Q4. Ask for their favorite verses.

Day Two

- Read Ezra 8 verses in sections. Ask Qs5-7 after each section.
- Read Ezra 8:32-36. Q8.
- Q9. Breakout session: How are you trusting God today for those things?

Day Three

- Read Ezra 9:1-5. Qs10&11.
- Read Ezra 9:8-9, 13, 15. Ask Q12. Read "Focus on the Meaning."
- Q13. Ask for their favorite verses.

Day Four

- Read Ezra 10:1-5, 7. Ask Qs14&15.
- Read Ezra 10:9-15. Q16.
- Q17. Ask for their favorite verses.

Other

- Discuss the podcast.
- Pray

Recommendation: Listen to a worship song such as "Lord I Need You," which fits very well with this study.

LESSON 8: NEHEMIAH 1-6

This lesson covers several chapters. Choose ahead of time which verses from the questions the group will read aloud as you proceed through the discussion. My recommendations are below.

Start with prayer.

Day One

- What grabbed their attention from the ABC's of Nehemiah?
- Read Ezra 7:13-14, 16, 21-23. This news led to Nehemiah's response.
- Read Nehemiah 1:2-6, 11. Qs1-3.
- Read Nehemiah 2:4-9. Qs4-6.
- Read Nehemiah 2:10-12, 17-20. Qs7-9.
- Q10. Ask for their favorite verses.

Day Two

- Do not read Nehemiah chapter 3. Ask Q11 and refer to verses the group mentions.
- Read Nehemiah 4 verses in sections. Ask Qs12-15 after each section.
- Read "Focus on the Meaning."
- Q16. Ask for their favorite verses.

Day Three

- Read Nehemiah 5:1-12. Qs17-19.
- Read Nehemiah 5:14-19. Q20. Read "Scriptural Insight."
- Q21. Ask for their favorite verses.

Day Four

- Read Nehemiah 6 in sections and ask Qs22-23 after each section.
- Qs24&25.
- Q26. Ask for their favorite verses.

Other

- Discuss the podcast.
- Pray

Recommendation: Listen to a worship song such as "Build My Life," which fits very well with this study.

LESSON 9: NEHEMIAH 7-13

This lesson covers several chapters. Choose ahead of time which verses from the questions the group will read aloud as you proceed through the discussion. My recommendations are below.

Start with prayer.

Day One

- Read Nehemiah 7:1-5. Qs1-4.

- Read Nehemiah 8 in sections and ask Qs5&6 after each section.

- Qs7&8.

- Q9. Ask for their favorite verses.

Day Two

- Read Nehemiah 9:1-3, 36-38. Qs10&11.

- Qs12&13.

- Q14. Ask for their favorite verses.

- Breakout session—briefly share your spiritual birth or commitment to follow Christ.

Day Three

- Read Nehemiah 10:28-29; skip the rest of the chapter. Qs15&16.

- Read Nehemiah 11:1-2. Q17.

- Read Nehemiah 12:27, 31, 38, 40, 43, 47. Qs18-20.

- Q21. Ask for their favorite verses.

Day Four

- Read Nehemiah 13 in sections and ask Qs22&23 after each section.

- Qs24&25.

- Q26. Ask for their favorite verses.

Other

- Discuss the podcast.

- Pray

Recommendation: Listen to a worship song such as "One Pure and Holy Passion," which fits very well with this study.

LESSON 10: MALACHI

This lesson covers several chapters. Choose ahead of time which verses from the questions the group will read aloud as you proceed through the discussion. My recommendations are below.

Start with prayer.

Day One

- Ask what grabbed their attention from the ABCs of Malachi.
- Read Malachi 1 by sections and ask Qs1-3 after each section.
- Q4. Ask for their favorite verses.

Day Two

- Read Malachi 2:1-6 in sections and ask Qs5-7 after each section.
- Read "Think About It."
- Q8. Ask for their favorite verses.

Day Three

- Read these verses in sections and ask Qs9-11 after each section.
- Talk about the beauty of Malachi 3:16.
- Q13. Ask for their favorite verses.

Day Four

- Read Malachi 4. Ask Qs14&15.
- Q16. Ask for their favorite verses.

Other

- Discuss the podcast.
- Pray

Recommendation: Listen to a worship song such as "Be unto Your Name," which fits very well with this study.

LESSON 11: DANIEL 9-12

This lesson covers several chapters. Choose ahead of time which verses from the questions the group will read aloud as you proceed through the discussion. My recommendations are below.

Start with prayer.

Day One

- Read Daniel 9:1-3. Q1.
- Read Daniel 9:17-19. Qs2&3.
- Read Daniel 9:20-24. Qs4-6. Ask for their favorite verses.

Day Two

- Read Daniel 10:1-7. Qs7&8.
- Read Daniel 10:8-11. Q9.
- Read Daniel 10:12-14. Q10. Discuss "Scriptural Insight."
- Read Daniel 10:15-17. Q11.
- Read Daniel 10:18-21. Q12. Discuss "Scriptural Insight."
- Q13. Ask for their favorite verses.

Day Three

- Read paragraph at top of page, "Daniel 11 is…"
- Read Daniel 11:32-35. Q14.
- Q15. Ask for their favorite verses.

Day Four

- Skip reading Daniel 11:36-45. Ask Q16.
- Read Daniel 12:1-3. Q17. Read "Scriptural Insight" and the verses at the end of it.
- Read the verses in Q18 in sections and answer the question.
- Q19.
- Qs20-21. Ask for their favorite verses.
- Discuss Q22.

Other

- Discuss the podcast.
- Pray

Recommendation: Listen to a worship song such as "Forever He Is Glorified," which fits very well with this study.

Sources

The following resources were used in the preparation and writing of this study.

1. Books of the Bible Chart by Teach Sunday School
2. Dr. Tom Constable, *Dr. Constable's Notes on Esther 2023 Edition*
3. Dr. Tom Constable, *Dr. Constable's Notes on Ezekiel 2023 Edition*
4. Dr. Tom Constable, *Dr. Constable's Notes on Ezra 2023 Edition*
5. Dr. Tom Constable, *Dr. Constable's Notes on Haggai 2023 Edition*
6. Dr. Tom Constable, *Dr. Constable's Notes on Jeremiah 2023 Edition*
7. Dr. Tom Constable, *Dr. Constable's Notes on Malachi 2023 Edition*
8. Dr. Tom Constable, *Dr. Constable's Notes on Nehemiah 2023 Edition*
9. Dr. Tom Constable, *Dr. Constable's Notes on Zechariah 2023 Edition*
10. John F. Walvoord and Roy B. Zuck, *The Bible Knowledge Commentary Old Testament,* Victor Books, 1983.
11. John F. Walvoord, "The Rise and Fall of Babylon," accessed at Bible.org.
12. Martin Luther, *What Luther Says: An Anthology*
13. Neo-Babylonian Empire map accessed at sturgiswesthistory.weebly.com
14. Persian Empire map accessed at reddit.com
15. The *NIV Study Bible New International Version*, Zondervan Bible Publishers, 1985.
16. Wayne Braudrick, *"God's Way of Communion"* podcast, 2/24/2022

www.ingramcontent.com/pod-product-compliance
Lightning Source LLC
Chambersburg PA
CBHW080751120626
46557CB00005B/1223